A catechist guide to the Traditional Latin Mass and Catholic Apologetics

---

Guy Breshears

<Published by Guy Breshears>

<2021>

First Printing: <2021>
ISBN: 978-988-77039-9-0

Other books by the author:
Loyal till Death: A Diary of the 13th New York Artillery
Major Granville Haller: Dismissed with Malice
To Seize Their Lands: Manifest Destiny in Washington State

Visit http://www.heritagebooks.com for more information of these books
Tales of a Traveler
Block Rosary: Hong Kong
Catholic answers: towards government and education
Visit http://www.lulu.com/spotlight/gbreshears for more information about these books

For more information about this book contact the publisher:
Guy Breshears
PO Box 88409
Sham Shui Po Post Office
Kowloon
Hong Kong

Dedication

To my wife who has stood by me ever since I have arrived in Hong Kong. I could not have survived without her continuing support.

Also, to Our Lady of China: Pray for all that live here so that those who govern will do so with equal justice for all. Finally, pray for the faithful who live here and have recourse to thee.

O God, who didst raise up the holy Confessor John Baptist to promote the Christian education of the poor and to confirm the young in thy way of truth, and, through him didst bring together a new family within Thy Church: mercifully grant through his prayers and example, that we may burn with zeal for Thy glory in the salvation of souls, and become worthy of a share of his heavenly crown.

-from the Collect of St. LaSalle, May 15

Table of Contents

INTRODUCTION

When one reads a definition of Mass it is usually: *Mass is the unbloody sacrifice of Calvary.* But what does it mean and why is Mass like Calvary? What is a sacrifice and why do we call Mass the Holy Sacrifice of Mass? Also, one often wonders if they have to pay attention to what the priest is doing at the altar.

A sacrifice is the offering of a victim, by a priest, to God alone to acknowledge that His is the Lord of all things. The act of sacrifice is an honor reserved to God alone since the formal act of offering and destroying a victim is an act of worship. The purpose of a sacrifice is: adoration, thanksgiving, petition and atonement.

Since the beginning of humanity sacrifices have been offered, by many religions, in order to give gratitude for gifts that have been received and to make petition. It wasn't until God gave Moses detailed instructions on sacrificial offerings that a true and correct form of offering was established (Lev 1-7,16,22).

While the sacrifices of the Old Law were pleasing to God they were far from perfect. In fact, God had expressed his desire to institute a far more perfect sacrifice which can be seen in the words of Malachias "From the rising of the sun even to the going down, my name is great among the Gentiles, and in every place there is sacrifice, and there is offered to my name a clean oblation." (Mal. 1:10-11)

At the Last Supper Christ instituted a new and visible sacrifice. He offered Himself to the Father as a sacrifice under the appearance of bread and wine. He told His Apostles to "Do this in remembrance of me" (Luke 22:19) and in doing so He choose to do this at the very time when the old sacrifice of the Paschal lamb was being celebrated.

Thus, the sacrifice of the Mass is the same sacrifice of the cross because the victim is the same and the principal Priest is the same– Jesus Christ. The Mass is the very same sacrifice (it is not just a remembrance of Christ's Passion) which was offered up at the Last Supper and consummated on

Calvary; it is a daily renewal of the sacrifice on the Cross. The only difference between the two is that Christ died once and can die no more. Therefore, at Mass Christ offers
Himself in an unbloody manner.

At Mass the priest speaks the words that have been given to us by Christ and handed down by the traditions of Holy Mother Church. Here you witness Christ reliving His sacrifice and you can see the entire Passion during Mass.

This introduction is to help the reader understand why Mass is the unbloody sacrifice of Calvary and why one must pay attention to what the priest is doing. It is my hope that by using this, along with a Missal, that one gains a better understanding and appreciation for the beauty and traditions of the Holy Sacrifice of the Mass.

Feast of St. John Baptist De LaSalle
Spokane, Washington

TYPES OF MASSES

A *High (or Solemn) Mass* is where a priest is assisted by a Deacon and a subdeacon; six or more candles are lighted on the Altar, incense and music are used, portions of the Mass are sung by the priest and his assistants, each singly and other portions by the choir.

A *Pontifical Mass* is a High Mass celebrated by a Bishop with special ceremonies.

A *Missa Cantata* is in the nature of a High Mass, and in churches where the clergy is insufficient, takes the place of a Solemn Mass. The celebrant sings certain parts but is not assisted by a Deacon or subdeacon and if incense is used, it is by privilege.

A *Low Mass* is one where the whole is read, not sung, by the celebrant. There is neither incense, liturgical singing, nor any of the solemnities of High Mass.

A *Parochial Mass* is the principal Mass, whether High or Low, on Sundays in a Parish Church.

A *Conventual Mass* is the Mass said or sung in conjunction with the Breviary Office, by the Chapter and Clergy of a Cathedral or Collegiate College, or the community of a Monastery or Convent.

A *Votive Mass* is one said, outside the Office of the day, for a particular purpose, public or private.

.

A *Requiem Mass* is a Mass said for the dead.

BRIEF HISTORY OF THE MASS

88- In a letter to the Corinthians Pope St. Clement wrote that Our Lord laid down the order of the Mass, referring to the Offertory, Consecration and Communion.

c.100- The Church adopts the Greek language for the Mass
155- In his writings St. Justin the Martyr says that after His Resurrection Our Lord taught the Apostles how to say Mass.

313- Edit of Milan states that the ceremonies and rituals for Mass are to be written down and not handed down by word of mouth.

360- St. Ambrose writes De Sacramentis, which quotes the central part of the Canon and is basically identical to what is used today.

380- The Church adopts Latin for the Mass.

600- Pope St. Gregory the Great finishes his Gregorian Sacramentary which is essentially the Mass 'codified' by Pope St. Pius V.

1442- Council of Florence declares the words to be used for the Consecration of the Body and Blood.

1570- Pope St. Pius V issues Quo Primum which specifies the exact Mass ritual for the Roman Rite.

Note: Since the 4th century only 26 words have been added to the Canon of the Mass. Thus, as the Council of Trent states the Canon is composed out of the very words of Our Lord, the tradition of the Apostles and the institutions of the Pontiffs.

PRAYER BEFORE MASS

Eternal Father, I unite myself with the intentions and affections of our Lady of Sorrows on Calvary, and I offer to Thee the Sacrifice which Thy beloved Son made of Himself on the Cross and which He now renews on this holy Altar. I offer it in the name of all mankind with the Masses which are now being offered, and all those which will be offered throughout the world this day:

To adore Thee and give Thee the honor which is due to Thee, confessing Thy supreme dominion over all things, and the absolute dependence of everything upon Thee, Who are our one and last End.

To thank Thee for the innumerable benefits we have received.

To appease Thy justice, aroused against us by so many sins, and to make satisfaction for them.

To implore grace and mercy for myself, for Thy Church, for all afflicted and sorrowing, for poor sinners, for those who I have promised prayers, for all the world and for the holy souls in Purgatory. Amen.

Each Holy Sacrifice of the Mass is offered in four parts:
Adoration, Thanksgiving, Reparation,
Petition

PRAYER OF ST. AMBROSE BEFORE HOLY COMMUION

O loving Lord Jesus Christ, I a sinner, presuming not on my own merits, but trusting in Thy mercy and goodness, with fear and trembling approach the table of Thy most sacred banquet. For I have defiled both my heart and body with many sins, and have not kept a strict guard over my mind and my tongue.

Wherefore, O gracious God, O awful Majesty, I, a wretched creature, entangled in difficulties, have recourse to Thee the font of mercy; to Thee do I fly that I may be healed, and take refuge under Thy protection, and I ardently desire to have Him as my Savior, Who I am unable to withstand as my Judge.

To Thee, O Lord, I show my wounds, to Thee I lay bare my shame. I know that my sins are many and great on account of which I am filled with fear. But I trust in Thy mercy, of which there is no end. Look down upon me, therefore, with the eyes of Thy mercy on me, who am full of misery and sin, Thou Who wilt never cease to let flow the fountain of mercy.

Hail, Victim of salvation, offered for me and for all mankind on the tree of the cross. Hail, noble and precious Blood, flowing from the wounds of my crucified Lord Jesus Christ and washing away the sins of the whole world. Remember, O Lord, Thy creature, who Thou hast redeemed with Thy Blood. I am grieved because I have sinned; I desire to make amends for what I have done.

Take away from me therefore, O most merciful Father, all my iniquities and sins, that being purified both in soul and body, I may worthily partake of the holy of holies; and grant that this holy oblation of Thy Body and Blood, of which though unworthy I purpose to partake, may be to me the remission of my sins, the perfect cleansing of my offenses, the means of driving away all evil thoughts and of renewing all holy desires, the accomplishments of works pleasing to Thee, as well as the strongest defense for soul and body against the snares of my enemies. Amen.

Stand

Hyssop is a tufted plant which the Jews used for ritual sprinkling

Every church has its own Guardian Angel

Sit while the priest vests for Mass

ASPERGES

said before a high Mass

P. Thou shalt sprinkle me, O Lord, with hyssop, and I shall be cleansed; Thou shalt wash me, and I shall become whiter than snow. Have mercy on me, O God, according to Thy great mercy. Glory be to the Father, and to the Son, and to the Holy Ghost.

S. As it was in the beginning, is now and ever shall be, world without end. Amen.

P. Thou shalt sprinkle me, O Lord, with hyssop, and I shall be cleanses: Thou shalt wash me, and I shall become whiter than snow. Show us, O Lord, Thy mercy.

S. And grant us Thy salvation

P. O Lord, hear my prayer.

S. And let my cry come unto Thee.

P. The Lord be with you.

S. And with thy spirit.

P. Let us pray. Hear us, O holy Lord, almighty Father, ever lasting God, and vouchsafe to send Thy holy Angel from heaven, to guard, cherish, protect, visit and defend all that are assembled in this place: Through Christ our Lord.

S. Amen.

said from Easter to Pentecost

P. I saw water flowing from the right side of the temple, alleluia; and all they to whom that water came were saved, and they shall say, alleluia, alleluia. Praise the Lord, for He is good; for His mercy endureth forever.

Stand when priest enters; Kneel when prayers begin
Jesus enters the Garden and begins to pray

This section is called Mass of the Catechumens because in the early Church those who weren't baptized could only be present until the end of the Sermon

In Masses for the Dead and from Passion Sunday till Holy Saturday this psalm is omitted

The priest reminds us of the significance of the Altar

The prayers said at the foot of the altar symbolize the thousands of years during which man was far from God, and longing for the Redeemer

MASS OF THE CATHECHUMENS

The priest, bowing down at the foot of the altar, makes the Sign of the Cross and says

P. In the Name of the Father, and of the Son† and of the Holy Ghost. Amen.

Then joining hands before his breast, he begins the Anthem

P. I will go in unto the altar of God.

S. To God who giveth joy to my youth.

JUDICA ME

P. Judge me, O God and distinguish my cause from the nation that is not holy: deliver me from the unjust and deceitful man.

S. For Thou, O God, art my strength: why hast Thou cast me off? And why go I sorrowful whilst the enemy afflicteth me?

P. Send forth Thy light and Thy truth: they have conducted me and brought me unto Thy holy mount, and into Thy tabernacles.

S. And I will go into the altar of God: to God, who giveth joy to my youth.

P. To Thee, O God, my God, I will give praise upon the harp; why art thou sad, O my soul, and why dost thou disquiet me?

S. Hope in God, for I will still give praise to Him: the salvation of my countenance and my God.

P. Glory be to the Father, and to the Son, and to the Holy Ghost.

S. As it was in the beginning, is now, and ever shall be, world without end. Amen.

The priest repeats the anthem

P. I will go in unto the altar of God.

S. To God, who giveth joy to my youth.

The priest, signing himself with the Sign of the Cross, says

P. Our help † is in the Name of the Lord.

S. Who made heaven and earth.

Jesus is prostrate in the Garden

The priest says the Confiteor as a preparation and as an expression of humility before God.

All cross themselves as the priest gives absolution

The priest, signing himself with the Sign of the Cross, says

P. Our help † is in the Name of the Lord.

S. Who made heaven and earth.

PUBLIC CONFESSION

Then, joining his hands, and humbly bowing down, he says the Confiteor

P. I confess to almighty God…

S. May almighty God be merciful to thee, and forgiving thy sins, bring thee to everlasting life.

P. Amen.

S. I confess to almighty God, to the blessed Mary ever Virgin, blessed Michael the Archangel, blessed John the Baptist, the holy Apostles Peter and Paul, to all the Saints, and to you Father, that I have sinned exceedingly in thought, word and deed, *(He strikes his breast three times)* through my fault, through my fault, through my most grievous fault. Therefore I beseech the blessed Mary, ever Virgin, blessed Michael the Archangel, blessed John the Baptist, the holy Apostles Peter and Paul, all the Saints, and you, Father, to pray to the Lord our God for me.

The priest, with his hands joined, says

P. May almighty God be merciful unto you, and forgiving you your sins, bring you to everlasting life.

S. Amen.

Signing himself with the Sign of the Cross, he says

P. May the † almighty and merciful Lord grant us pardon, absolution, and remission of our sins.

S. Amen

The priest makes a final plea to God that he may go up to the Altar with a pure soul

Judas betrays Jesus with a kiss

The early Church offered Mass on the tombs of martyrs; thus associating their sacrifice with Christ's

Jesus is dragged to prison and receives a blow

Bowing down, he proceeds
P. O God, Thou wilt turn again and quicken us.
S. And thy people shall rejoice in Thee.
P. Show us, O Lord, Thy mercy.
S. And grant us Thy salvation.
P. O Lord, hear my prayer.
S. And let my cry come unto Thee.
P. The Lord be with you.
S. And with thy spirit.
P. Let us pray.

PRIEST ASCENDS THE ALTAR

First extending, then joining his hands, the priest audibly says Oremus*; then ascending to the altar, he says secretly*

P. Take away from us our iniquities, we beseech Thee, O Lord, that we may be worthy to enter with pure minds into the Holy of Holies, through Christ our Lord. Amen.

His hands, joined, and bowing down over the altar, the priest says

We beseech Thee, O Lord, by the merits of Thy Saints, (*he kisses the sacred stone)* whose relics are here, and of all the Saints, that Thou wouldst vouchsafe to forgive me all my sins. Amen.

INTROIT

The priest, signing himself with the Sign of the Cross, reads the Introit of the day

Jesus is 3 times denied by St. Peter

This is the only part of Mass said in Greek

This prayer is repeated nine times:
Three times for God the Father,
Three times for God the Son,
Three times for God the Holy Ghost

The Gloria is the Church's greatest hymn of praise.
It gives honor and glory to the Blessed Trinity

Jesus looks at St. Peter and touches his heart

KYRIE ELEISON

Then, joining his hands, he says alternately, with the server

P. Lord, have mercy
S. Lord, have mercy
P. Lord, have mercy
S. Christ, have mercy
P. Christ, have mercy
S. Christ, have mercy
P. Lord, have mercy
S. Lord, have mercy
P. Lord, have mercy

GLORIA IN EXCELSIS

Omitted during Lent, Advent and Masses for the Dead

P. Glory be to God on high, and on earth peace to men of good will. We praise Thee. We bless Thee. We adore Thee. We glorify Thee. We give Thee thanks for Thy great glory. O Lord God, heavenly King, God the Father almighty. O Lord Jesus Christ, the only
begotten Son. O Lord God, Lamb of God, Son of the Father. Who takest away the sins of the world,
have mercy on us. Who takest away the sins of the world, receive our prayer. Who sittest at the right hand of the Father, have mercy on us. For Thou only art holy. Thou only art the Lord. Thou only art most high, O Jesus Christ. Together with the Holy Ghost † in the glory of God the Father. Amen

The priest kisses the altar, turns to the people and says

P. The Lord be with you.
S. And with thy spirit.

This is the collected prayers of all the faithful assisting at the Holy Sacrifice of the Mass

COLLECT

The priest reads the Collect of the day

P. Let us pray.

At the end of the Collect the server answers

S. Amen

Sit

Jesus is led to Pilate

Jesus is led to Herod

After the Gradual the Missal is carried to the Gospel side of the altar which symbolizes the passing of the faith from the Jews to the Gentiles

This is a prayer of preparation before reading the Gospel

Stand

Jesus is mocked as a fool and sent back to Pilate

EPISTLE

The priest reads the Epistle of the day;at the end of the Epistle the server answers

S. Thanks be to God.

GRADUAL

The priest reads the Gradual, Tract or Alleluia of the day

P. Cleanse my heart and my lips, O Almighty God, who didst cleanses the lips of the prophet Isaias with a burning coal, and vouchsafe, through Thy
gracious mercy, so to purify me, that I may worthily announce Thy holy Gospel. Through Christ, Our Lord. Amen.

P. Give me Thy blessing, O. Lord. The Lord be in my heart and on my lips, that I may worthily and in becoming manner, proclaim His holy Gospel. Amen

P. The Lord be with you.

S. And with thy spirit.

GOSPEL

The priest reads the Gospel of the day

P. The continuation (or beginning) of the holy Gospel according to N…

The priest signs the Book, and himself on the forehead, mouth and breast. The server says

S. Glory be to Thee, O Lord.

At the end of the Gospel the server answers:

S. Praise be to Thee, O Christ.

The priest kisses the Gospel and says:

P. By the words of the Gospel may our sins be blotted out.

Stand

The Nicene Creed is one of the most ancient expressions of the Catholic Faith. It is said on all Sundays and other major feastdays

Sit

Jesus is stripped of His Garments and is scourged

NICENE CREED

P. I believe in one God, the Father almighty, Maker of heaven and earth, and of all things, visible and invisible. And in one Lord Jesus Christ, the only begotten Son of God. And born of the Father, before all ages. God of God: Light of Light: true God of true God. Begotten, not made, consubstantial with the Father, by whom all things were made. Who, for us men, and for our salvation, came down from heaven. (*Here all kneel*) **AND BECAME INCARNATE BY THE HOLY GHOST OF THE VIRGIN MARY: AND WAS MADE MAN**. He was crucified also for us, suffered under Pontius Pilate, and was buried. And the third day He rose again according to the Scriptures. And ascended into heaven, and sitteth at the right hand of the Father. And He shall come again with glory to judge both the living and the dead, of whose kingdom there shall be no end. And in the Holy Ghost, the Lord and Giver of Life, proceeding from the Father and the Son. Who together, with the Father and the Son, is adored and glorified: Who spoke by the prophets. And in one, holy, Catholic and Apostolic Church. I confess one baptism for the remission of sins. And look for the resurrection of the dead. † And the life of the world to come. Amen.

MASS OF THE FAITHFUL

OFFERTORY

The priest kisses the altar and turns towards the people and says

P. The Lord be with you.

S. And with thy spirit.

P. Let us pray.

Then the priest reads the Offertory

The wine and water represent the two natures of Christ

A few drops of water are poured into the wine in remembrance of the water and blood which flowed from the side of Jesus

OFFERING OF BREAD AND WINE

The priest takes the paten with the host and offering it up says

P. Accept, O holy Father, almighty and eternal God, this unspotted host, which I, Thy unworthy servant, offer unto Thee, my living and true God, for my innumerable sins, offenses, and negligences, and for all here present: as also for all faithful Christians, both living and dead, that it may avail both me and them for salvation unto life everlasting. Amen.

Making the Sign of the Cross with the paten, the priest places the host upon the corporal. He pours wine and water into the chalice, blessing the water before it is mixed.

P. O God, † who, in creating human nature, didst wonderfully dignify it, and still more wonderfully restore it, grant that, by the Mystery of this water and wine, we may be made partakers of His divine nature, who vouchsafed to be made partaker of our human nature, even Jesus Christ our Lord, Thy Son, who with Thee, liveth and reignth in the unity of the Holy Ghost, God: world without end. Amen.

Then the priest takes the chalice and offers it saying

P. We offer unto Thee, O Lord, the chalice of salvation, beseeching Thy clemency, that it may ascend before Thy divine Majesty, as a sweet savor, for our salvation, and for that of the whole world. Amen.

The priest makes the Sign of the Cross with the chalice, places it upon the corporal, and covers it with the pall. Then with his hands joined upon the altar, and bowing down slightly he says

P. Accept us, O Lord, in the spirit of humility and contrition of heart, and grant that the sacrifice which we offer this day in Thy sight may be pleasing to Thee, O Lord God.

The priest implores God that the sacrifice may be acceptable to Him and he calls upon the Holy Ghost to bless it

Pilate washes his hands

The priest washes his fingers to symbolize the purity and and cleanliness of all who offer or take part in the
Sacrifice

The Glory is not used in Masses of the Dead and Passiontide

Jesus is crowned with thorns

This prayer of offering to the Holy Trinity states in detail the purpose for which the Sacrifice is offered

Raising his eyes towards heaven, extending and then joining his hands, the priest makes the Sign of the Cross over the host and chalice and invokes the Holy Ghost by saying

P. Come, O almighty and eternal God, the Sanctifier and bless† this Sacrifice, prepared for the glory of Thy holy Name.

WASHING OF THE HANDS

P. I will wash my hands among the innocent: and I will compass Thine altar O Lord, That I may hear the voice of praise: and tell of all Thy wondrous works. I have loved, O Lord, the beauty of Thy house and the place where Thy glory dwelleth. Take not away my soul, O God, with the wicked: nor my life with blood-thirsty men. In whose hands are iniquities, their right hand is filled with gifts. But I have walked in my innocence: redeem me, and have mercy on me. My foot hath stood in the direct way, in the churches I will bless Thee, O Lord. Glory to the Father and….

PRAYER TO THE MOST HOLY TRINITY

Bowing down before the middle of the altar, the priest with joined hands says

P. Receive, O holy Trinity, this oblation which we make to Thee, in memory of the Passion, Resurrection and Ascension of our Lord Jesus Christ and in honor of Blessed Mary, ever Virgin, blessed John the Baptist, the holy Apostles Peter and Paul and of all the Saints, that it may avail unto their honor and our salvation and may they vouchsafe to intercede for us in heaven whose memory we celebrate on earth. Through the same Christ our Lord. Amen.

Pilate says to the Jews “Behold the Man”

Feeling unworthy the priest turns to the people and asks for their prayers.

The Secret is said inaudibly because the priest acts as a mediator to God on behalf of man. This is the completion of the Offertory prayers

Jesus is condemned to death

Kneel

Jesus enters Jerusalem

The bells are rung three times♪♪♪

ORATE FRATRES

The priest kisses the altar and turns towards the people and audibly says

P. Brethren, pray that my Sacrifice and yours may be acceptable to God the Father almighty.

S. May the Lord receive the Sacrifice from thy hands to the praise and glory of His Name, to our benefit and that of all His holy Church.

P. Amen.

SECRET

With outstretched hands, the priest recites the Secret then says

P. World without end.

S. Amen.

PREFACE

P. The Lord be with you.

S. And with thy spirit.

P. Lift up your hearts.

S. We have them lifted up to the Lord.

P. Let us give thanks to the Lord our God.

S. It is meet and just.

The priest then disjoins his hands and keeps them this way until the end of the Preface; afterwards he again joins them and bowing down says Sanctus. When he says Benedictus, he blesses himself.

SANCTUS

P. Holy, holy, holy, Lord God of Hosts! Heaven and earth are full of Thy glory! Hosanna in the highest! Blessed is He that cometh in the Name of the Lord. Hosanna in the highest!

This starts the Canon of the Mass

If there is a vacancy in the Holy See of Rome or in the local diocese then the reference to the Pope or Bishop is eliminated until that position is filled

Jesus carries His cross

In union with the priest mention here the names for which you offer the Divine Victim

Veronica wipes the face of Jesus

The priest venerates the members of the Church Triumphant and implores their assistance. This concludes the opening prayers of the Canon

PRAYERS BEFORE THE CONSECRATION

FOR THE CHURCH

P. We therefore, humbly pray and beseech Thee, most merciful Father, through Jesus Christ; Thy Son, our Lord, *(he kisses the altar)* that Thou wouldst vouchsafe to accept and bless these † gifts, these† presents, these† holy unspotted Sacrifices, which in the first place we offer Thee for Thy holy Catholic Church to which vouchsafe to grant peace, as also to preserve, unite and govern it throughout the world, together with Thy servant N. our Pope and N. our Bishop and all orthodox believers and professors of the Catholic and Apostolic Faith.

COMMEMORATION OF THE LIVING

P. Be mindful, O Lord, of Thy servants and handmaidens, N. and N. and of all here present whose faith and devotion are known unto Thee, for whom we offer, or who offer up to Thee this sacrifice of praise for themselves, their families and friends, for the redemption of their souls, for the health and salvation they hope for; and who now pay their vows to Thee, the everlasting, living and true God.

INVOCATION OF THE SAINTS

P. Communicating with and honoring in the first place the memory of the glorious ever Virgin Mary, Mother of our Lord and God Jesus Christ: as also of the blessed Apostles and Martyrs Peter and Paul, Andrew, James, John, Thomas, James, Philip, Bartholomew, Matthew, Simon and Thaddeus: Linus, Cletus, Clement, Xystus, Cornelius, Cyprian, Lawrence, Chrysogonus, John and Paul, Cosmas and Damian and of all Thy Saints, through whose merits and prayers, grant that we may in all things be defended by the help of Thy protection. Through the same Christ our Lord. Amen.

The bells are rung once♪

Jesus is nailed to the cross

The cross is elevated between heaven and earth

PRAYERS AT THE CONSECRATION
OBLATION OF THE VICTIM TO GOD

P. We therefore beseech Thee, O Lord, graciously to accept this oblation of our service, as also of Thy whole family; and to dispose our days in Thy peace, preserve us from eternal damnation and rank us in the number of Thine Elect. Through Christ our Lord. Amen.

P. Which oblation do Thou, O God, vouchsafe in all respects, to bless, † approve, † ratify, †make worthy and acceptable; that it may be made for us the Body† and Blood† of thy most beloved Son Jesus Christ our Lord.

CONSECRATION OF THE HOST

P. Who, the day before He suffered, took bread into His holy and venerable hands, and with His eyes lifted up towards heaven unto Thee, God, His almighty Father, giving thanks to Thee, He blessed† it, broke it and gave it to His disciples saying: Take and eat ye all of this ***FOR THIS IS MY BODY***

After pronouncing the words of Consecration, the priest kneeling adores the Sacred Host ♪; rising he elevates It ♪; genuflects and adores It again ♪. Look at the Sacred Host with faith, piety and love saying: "My Lord and My God!"

The Blood of Jesus flows from His wounds

CONSECRATION OF THE WINE

Then, uncovering the wine the priest says

P. In like manner, after He had supped, taking also this excellent chalice into His holy and venerable hands, and giving Thee thanks, He blessed†, and gave to His disciples saying: Take and drink ye all of this.

FOR THIS IS THE CHALICE OF MY BLOOD OF THE NEW AND ETERNAL TESTAMENT, THE MYSTERY OF FAITH; WHICH SHALL BE SHED FOR YOU AND FOR MANY UNTO THE REMISSION FOR SINS

Then the priest says in a low voice:

P. As often as ye do these things, ye shall do them in remembrance of Me.

The priest kneels and adores the Precious Blood ♪; rising he elevates the Chalice♪ and setting it down he covers it and adores it again ♪.

OBLATION OF THE VICTIM TO GOD

P. Wherefore, O Lord, we Thy servants, as also Thy holy people, calling to mind the blessed Passion of the same Christ, Thy Son, our Lord, and also His Resurrection from the dead and His glorious Ascension into heaven: do offer unto Thy most excellent Majesty of Thine own gifts, bestowed upon us, a pure† Host, a holy† Host, an unspotted† Host, the holy† Bread of eternal life and the Chalice† of everlasting salvation.

The sacrifices of the Old Law prefigure the Sacrifice of the New Law

The section completes the prayers for members of the Mystical Body of Christ

Extending his hands, he proceeds

P. Upon which vouchsafe to look with a propitious and serene countenance and to accept them as Thou wert graciously pleased to accept the gifts of Thy just servant Abel, and the sacrifice of our patriarch Abraham and that which Thy high priest Melchisedech offered to Thee, a holy Sacrifice, an unspotted victim.

Bowing down, with his hands joined and placed upon the altar he continues:

P. We most humbly beseech Thee, almighty God, command these offerings to be born by the hands of Thy holy Angels to Thine altar on high, in the sight of Thy divine Majesty, that as many *(he kisses the altar)* as shall partake of the most holy Body† and Blood† of Thy Son at this altar may be filled with every heavenly grace and blessing. Through the same Christ our Lord. Amen.

PRAYERS AFTER THE CONSECRATION

FOR THE DEAD

P. Remember also, O Lord, Thy servants and handmaidens N. and N., who are gone before us with the sign of faith and rest in the sleep of peace. To these, O Lord, and to all that rest in Christ grant we beseech Thee a place of refreshment, light and peace; Through the same Christ our Lord. Amen.

The conversion of the thief

These are the only words in the Canon which the priest says in a somewhat elevated voice, to symbolize an act of public self-humiliation

The seven words of Jesus

INVOCATION OF THE SAINTS

P. To us also, Thy sinful servants, confiding in the multitude of Thy mercies vouchsafe to grant some part and fellowship with Thy holy Apostles and Martyrs, with John, Stephen, Matthias, Barnabas, Ignatius, Alexander, Marcellinus, Peter, Felicitas, Perpetua, Agatha, Lucy, Agnes, Cecilia, Anastasia and with all Thy Saints into whose company we beseech Thee to admit us not weighing our merits but pardoning our offenses. Through Christ our Lord.

MINOR ELEVATION

P. By whom, O Lord, Thou dost ever create, sanctify, † quicken, † bless, † and give unto us all these good things. By Him, † and with Him, † and in Him † is to Thee, God the Father† almighty, in unity of the Holy† Ghost, all honor and glory. World without end.

S. Amen.

THE COMMUNION

P. Let us pray. Instructed by Thy saving precepts and following Thy divine institution, we are bold to say

P. Our Father, who art in heaven, hallowed be Thy Name; Thy kingdom come; Thy will be done on earth as it is in heaven. Give us this day our daily bread. And forgive us our trespasses as we forgive those who trespass against us. And lead us not into temptation.

S. But deliver us from evil.

P. Amen.

This prayer expands the final words of the Lord's Prayer

Jesus expires on the cross

The soul of Jesus descends into Limbo

LIBERA NOS AND THE DIVISION OF THE HOST

The priest takes the paten between the first and second fingers and says

P. Deliver us, we beseech Thee, O Lord, from all evils, past, present and to come; and by the intercession of the Blessed and glorious ever Virgin Mary, Mother of God and of the holy Apostles Peter and Paul and of Andrew and of all the Saints (*He signs himself with the paten and kisses it)* mercifully grant peace in our days that through the assistance of Thy mercy we may be always free from sin and secure from all disturbance.

He places the paten under the Host, uncovers the Chalice and makes a genuflection; rising he takes the Host, breaks It in the middle over the Chalice saying

P. Through the same Jesus Christ, Thy Son, our Lord.

He breaks off a Particle from the divided Host

P. Who with Thee in the unity of the Holy Ghost liveth and reignth God, World without end.

S. Amen.

MIXTURE OF THE BODY AND BLOOD

The priest makes the Sign of the Cross with the Particle over the Chalice saying:

P. The peace† of the Lord be† always with† you.

S. And with they spirit.

He puts the Particle into the Chalice saying

P. May this mixture and consecration of the Body and Blood of our Lord Jesus Christ be to us who receive it effectual unto eternal life. Amen.

The conversion of many

In Masses for the Dead the priest says twice:
Grant them rest and then lastly:
Grant them eternal rest

In the Old Law an unblemished lamb was used to atone for sin. In the New Law, Christ, the heavenly Lamb, takes away the sins of the world

In Mass for the Dead this prayer is not used

AGNUS DEI

The priest covers the Chalice, genuflects and rises; then bowing down and striking his breast three times, he says:

P. Lamb of God who takest away the sins of the world, have mercy on us.

P. Lamb of God who takest away the sins of the world have mercy on us.

P. Lamb of God who takest away the sins of the world, grant us peace.

PRAYERS FOR HOLY COMMUNION

PRAYER FOR PEACE

P. O Lord Jesus Christ, who saidst to Thine Apostles: Peace I leave you, My peace I give you: regard not my sins, but the faith of Thy Church; and vouchsafe to grant her that peace and unity which is agreeable to Thy will: Who livest and reignest God, world without end. Amen.

PRAYER FOR SANCTIFICATION

P. O Lord Jesus Christ, Son of the living God, who according to the will of Thy Father, with the cooperation of the Holy Ghost hast by Thy death given life to the world; deliver me by this Thy most sacred Body and Blood from all my iniquities and from all evils; and make me always cleave to Thy commandments and suffer me never to be separated from Thee, Who livest and reignest, with the same God the Father and the Holy Ghost, God, world without end. Amen.

PRAYER FOR GRACE

P. Let not the partaking of Thy Body, O Lord, Jesus Christ, which I, though unworthy, presume to receive turn to my judgment and condemnation; but let it, through Thy mercy, become a safeguard and remedy, both for soul and body; Who with God the Father, in the unity of the Holy Ghost, livest and reignest God, for ever and ever. Amen.

Jesus is buried

The bells are rung three times ♪♪♪

This recalls the Centurion's humble prayer

In the soul of the priest, as in that of every faithful who communicates, there is a predominate feeling of thanksgiving

COMMUNION OF THE PRIEST

COMMUNION OF THE BODY

The priest genuflects, rises and says

P. I will take the Bread of heaven and will call upon the Name of the Lord.

Raising his voice a little the priest says three times

P. Lord, I am not worthy that Thou shouldst enter under my roof; say but the word, and my soul shall be healed.

Then with his right hand, making the Sign of the Cross with the Host over the paten he says

P. The Body of our Lord Jesus Christ preserve my soul unto life everlasting. Amen. (*He then reverently receives both halves of the Host)*

COMMUNION OF THE BLOOD

The priest then uncovers the Chalice, genuflects, collects whatever fragments may remain on the corporal and purifies the paten over the Chalice saying

P. What return shall I make the Lord for all He has given me? I will take the chalice of salvation and call upon the Name of the Lord. Praising I will call upon the Lord, and I shall be saved from my enemies. (*The priest takes the Chalice and making the Sign of the Cross with it saying)* The Blood of our Lord Jesus Christ preserve my soul unto life everlasting. Amen. (*The priest receives all the Precious Blood, together with the Particle)*

COMMUNION OF THE FAITHFUL

If Holy Communion is to be distributed, the server says the Confiteor. After which the priest says

P. May almighty God have mercy upon you, forgive you your sins and bring you unto life everlasting.

S. Amen.

In order to receive Communion you must be a baptized Catholic and without mortal sin

If you do not receive Communion then you should make a spiritual communion

Jesus is embalmed

The priest prays that God will permit His gifts to have enduring effects in the souls of all those who have partaken Communion

The Resurrection of Jesus and appears to His Disciples

Making the Sign of the Cross the priest continues

P. May the almighty and merciful Lord grant you pardon,† absolution and remission of your sins.

S. Amen.

Elevating a Particle of the Blessed Sacrament and turning towards the people the priest says

P. Behold the Lamb of God, behold Him who taketh away the sins of the world. *(And then he says three times)* Lord I am not worthy that Thou shouldst enter under my roof; say but the word and my soul shall be healed.

The priest then gives communion saying to each

The Body of our Lord Jesus Christ preserve thy soul unto life everlasting. Amen.

PRAYERS DURING THE ABLUTIONS

P. Grant, O Lord, that what we have taken with our mouth we may receive with a pure mind; and from a temporal gift may it become to us an eternal remedy.

The priest holds the Chalice to the server who pours wine into it for the first ablution

P. May Thy Body, O Lord, which I have received and Thy Blood which I have drunk cling to my inmost being; and grant that no stain of sin may remain in me who have been fed with this pure and holy Sacrament; Who livest and reignest for ever and ever. Amen.

The priest washes his fingers and receives the second ablution

Jesus converses for 40 days with His Disciples

Jesus sends His Apostles to evangelize the world and ascends into Heaven

If the Gloria in excelsis has not been said there
is said instead of the Ite, Missa est:
P. Let us bless the Lord
S. Thanks be to God.

The descent of the Holy Ghost

The prayer that follows the dismissal is a petition to God to make the Sacrifice useful to the priest and the faithful

COMMUNION VERSE

The priest kisses the altar

P. The Lord be with you.

S. And with thy spirit.

P. Let us pray. *(The priest reads the communion verse)*

POST COMMUNION VERSE

The priest reads the post verse and the server answers

S. Amen

CONCLUSION OF THE MASS

DISMISSAL

P. The Lord be with you.

S. And with thy spirit.

P. Go, the Mass is ended.

S. Thanks be to God.

BLESSING

P. May the performance of my homage be pleasing to Thee, O holy Trinity: and grant that the Sacrifice which I, though unworthy, have offered up in the sight of Thy Majesty may be acceptable to Thee, and through Thy mercy, be a propitiation for me and for all those for whom I have offered it. Through Christ our Lord. Amen.

The priest turns to the faithful, invoking upon them the blessing of God and making over them the Sign of the Cross

P. May almighty God the Father, Son, † and Holy Ghost bless you.

S. Amen.

Stand

It is proper that the last word of the Mass should be one of thanksgiving

LAST GOSPEL

P. The Lord be with you.

S. And with thy spirit.

P. The beginning† of the holy Gospel according to John.

S. Glory be to Thee, O Lord.

P. In the beginning was the Word, and the Word was with God, and the Word was God. The same was in the beginning with God. All things were made by Him, and without Him was made nothing that was made: in Him was life, and the life was the Light of men; and the Light shineth in darkness, and the darkness did not comprehend it. There was a man sent from God, whose name was John. This man came for a witness, to testify concerning the Light, that all might believe through Him. He was not the Light, but he was to testify concerning the Light. That was the true Light, which enlighteneth every man that cometh into this world. He was in the world, and the world was made by Him, and the world knew Him not. He came unto His own, and His own received Him not. But as many as received Him to them He gave power to become sons of God, to them that believe in His Name, who are born not of blood, nor of the will of the flesh, nor of the will of man, but of God. *(Here all kneel)* **AND THE WORD WAS MADE FLESH**,and dwelt among us: and we saw His glory, the glory as of the Only begotten of the Father, full of grace and truth.

S. Thanks be to God.

PRAYERS AFTER MASS

For the conversion of Russia and for the triumph of Holy Mother Church. To be said kneeling

P. Hail Mary, full of grace, the Lord is with thee; blessed art thou among women, and blessed is the Fruit of thy womb, Jesus.
All. Holy Mary, Mother of God, pray for us sinners, now and at the hour of our death. Amen. *(said 3 times)*

All. Hail, Holy Queen, Mother of Mercy, our life, our sweetness and our hope. To thee do we cry poor banished children of Eve. To thee do we send up our sighs, mourning and weeping in this vale of tears. Turn then, most gracious Advocate, thine eyes of mercy towards us. And after this our exile show unto us the blessed Fruit of they womb, Jesus. O clement, O loving, O sweet Virgin Mary.
P. Pray for us, O holy Mother of God.
All. That we may be worthy of the promises of Christ.

P. Let us pray. O God, our refuge and our strength, look down with favor upon Thy people who cry to Thee; and by the intercession of the glorious and Immaculate Virgin Mary, Mother of God, of St. Joseph her Spouse, of Thy blessed Apostles Peter and Paul, and of the Saints, mercifully and graciously hear the prayers which we pour forth for the conversion of sinners, and for the liberty and exaltation of holy Mother the Church. Through the same Christ our Lord.
All. Amen.

All. Saint Michael the Archangel, defend us in battle; be our protection against the wickedness and snares of the devil. May God rebuke him, we humbly pray: and do thou, O Prince of the heavenly host, by the power of God, cast into hell Satan and all the evil spirits who wander about seeking the ruin of souls. Amen.

P. Most Sacred Heart of Jesus
All. Have mercy on us *(said 3 times)*

PRAYERS AFTER HOLY COMMUNION
Prayers after receiving Holy Communion

Prayer of St. Thomas Aquinas

I give Thee thanks, holy Lord, Father almighty, everlasting God, who hast vouchsafed to fee me, a sinner, Thine unworthy servant, for no merits of my own, but only out of the goodness of Thy great mercy, with the precious Body and Blood of Thy Son, our Lord Jesus Christ; and I pray Thee, that this holy communion may be to me, not guilt for punishment, but a saving intercession for pardon. Let it be to me an armor of faith and a shield of good-will. Let it be to me a casting out of vices; a driving away of all evil desires and fleshly lusts; an increase of charity, patience, humility, obedience, and all virtues; a firm defense against the plots of my enemies, both seen and unseen; a perfect quieting of all motions of sin, both in my flesh and in my spirit; a firm cleaving unto Thee, the only and true God, and a happy ending to my life. And I pray Thee to deign to bring me, a sinner, to that ineffable Feast, where Thou with Thy Son and the Holy Ghost, art to Thy holy ones true light, full satisfaction, everlasting joy, consummate pleasure and perfect happiness. Amen.

O Lord Jesus Christ, Son of the living God, who according to the will of the Father, with the cooperation of the Holy Ghost, hast by Thy death given life unto the world, deliver me by Thy most sacred Body, which I, unworthy, have presumed to receive, from all my iniquities and from ever evil, and make me ever to hold fast to Thy commandments and suffer me never to be separated from Thee. Amen.

Prayers of Spiritual Communion

Prayer of St. Alphonsus Liguori

My Jesus, I believe that Thou art present in the Blessed Sacrament. I love Thee above all things and I desire Thee in my soul. Since I cannot now receive Thee sacramentally, come at least spiritually into my heart. As though thou wert already there, I embrace Thee and unit myself wholly to Thee; permit me not that I should never be separated from Thee. Amen.

At Thy feet, O my Jesus, I prostrate myself and I offer Thee the repentance of my contrite heart, which is humbled in its nothingness and in Thy holy presence. I adore Thee in the Sacrament of Thy love, the ineffable Eucharist. I desire to receive Thee into the poor dwelling that my heart offers Thee. While waiting for the happiness of sacramental Communion, I wish to possess Thee in spirit. Come to me, O my Jesus, since I, for my part, am coming to Thee! May Thy love embrace my whole being in life and in death. I believe in Thee, I hope in Thee, I love Thee. Amen.

SAINTS OF THE MASS

Saints named before the Consecration
As found in the prayer Communicating and after the Apostles are named

St. Linus- Pope, Martyr; The successor of St. Peter in the Apostolic See and ruled the Church for about nine years. He was martyred and was buried next to St. Peter in the year 78. Feast day is September 23

St. Cletus- Pope, Martyr; Succeed St. Linus and was martyred under Domitian in the year 91. Feast day is April 26

St. Clement- Pope, Martyr; Succeed St. Cletus, was a companion to Sts. Peter and Paul and was exiled by the emperor Trajan and cast into the sea in the year 100. Feast day is November 23

St. Sixtus- Pope, Martyr; Succeed St. Clement and was martyred about the year 125. Feast day is April 6

St. Cornelius- Pope, Martyr; Succeed St. Fabian and was beheaded in the year 253. Feast day is September 16

St. Cyprian- Bishop, Martyr; Was the Archbishop of Carthage and Primate of Africa and was martyred in the year 258. Feast day is September 16

St. Lawrence- Deacon, Martyr; When he was arrested in Rome he gave away the possessions of the Church to the poor to save them from confiscation. He was martyred in the year 258. Feast day is August 10

St. Chrysogonus- Martyr; Arrested in Rome and was beheaded in the year 303. Feast day is November 24

Sts. John and Paul- Martyrs; Two brothers who were officers under

Constantinus. After the death of this Christian emperor they became martyrs at Rome in the persecution of Julian the Apostate in the year 362. Feast day is June 26

Sts. Cosmas and Damian- Martyrs; Two brothers who were beheaded in Cicilia, under Diocletian, by the order of the prefect Lysias in the year 283. Feast day is September 27

Saints named after the Consecration
As found in the prayer To us also

St. John the Baptist- Martyr; The Precursor of Christ who lead an austere life as a hermit, announced the Advent of Christ, preached penitence, baptized in the Jordan and was beheaded during the reign of Herod. Feasts days are June 23,24, August 29

St. Stephen- Protomartyr; One of the seven Deacons chosen by the Apostles to help them and was renowned for his virtues, wonders and signs that the Jews summoned him before the Sanhedrin and was stoned to death. Feast day is December 26

St. Matthias- Apostle, Martyr; One of the 72 disciples of Jesus and chosen to replace Judas and preached in Judea, Cappadocia, Egypt and Ethiopia before being stoned to death by the Jews in the year 80. Feast day is February 24 or 25 (in a leap year)

St. Barnabas- Apostle, Martyr; Companion of St. Paul and was given the title of Apostle by his preaching and labors before being stoned to death by the Jews about the year 61. Feast day is June 11
St. Ignatius of Antioch- Bishop, Martyr; A disciple of St. John the Apostle who was sent to Rome in chains, condemned to the wild beasts and died in the year 110. Feast day is February 1

St. Alexander I- Pope, Martyr; Fifth Pope after St. Peter who was beheaded outside of Rome on the Nomentan Way together with the priests Eventius and Theodulus. Feast day is May 3

Sts. Marcellinus and St. Peter- Martyrs; both suffered fearful torments and were beheaded in 302. Feast day is June 2

Sts. Felicita and Perpetua- Martyrs; These two young mothers, the former a lady of high rank and the other a slave were arrested at Carthage along with other Christians and were condemned to the wild beasts and finally by the sword in the year 202. Feast day is March 6

St. Agatha- Virgin, Martyr; Born in Sicily of noble parents and suffered dreadful torture at the hands of her persecutors, but was healed by St. Peter on the following night, and then suffered more and died in the year 254. Feast day is February 5

St. Lucy- Virgin, Martyr; Born in Sicily of noble parents, gave herself to Jesus and chose death rather than lose the incorruptible treasure of her virginity in the year 303. Feast day is December 13

St. Agnes- Virgin, Martyr; Was beheaded at the age of 13 rather than lose the treasure of her virginity in the year 304. Feast day is January 21

St. Cecilia- Virgin, Martyr; Converted her husband and brother-in-law, preserved her virginity and was beheaded in the year 230. Feast day is November 22

St. Anastasia- Widow, Martyr; After the death of her husband she gave herself over to the practices of charity and mercy and was martyred by fire in the year 303. Feast day is December 25

SACRED VESSELS OF THE MASS
Altar Stone- Signifies Mount Calvary

Altar Cloths- Signifies the burial clothes of Jesus

Steps before the Altar- Signifies the Mount of Olives on the way to Calvary
Missal- Signifies the book of death which was canceled by the sacrifice of Jesus

The 2 Cruets- Signifies the sponge filled with gall and vinegar given to Jesus on the cross

Chalice- Represents the tomb Jesus was laid in

Chalice Cloth- Represents the mantle of Jesus

Paten- Represents the grave stone

Purificator- Represents the handkerchief covering the face of Jesus for burial

Corporal- Represents the grave clothes of Jesus

VESTMENTS OF THE MASS
The *Amice* is a piece of white linen cloth which covers the priest shoulders and represents the cloth that covered the face of Jesus. The vesting prayer is "Place, O Lord, on my head the helmet of salvation, that I may overcome the assaults of the devil."

The *Alb* is a white linen tunic which covers the priest's whole body and represents the garment of vesture Herod caused to be put on Jesus. The vesting prayer is "Purify me, O Lord, from all stain and cleanse my heart, that washed in the Blood of the Lamb, I may enjoy eternal delights."

The *Cincture* is the cord which fastens the alb at the waist and represents the rope with which Jesus was bound for scourging. The vesting prayer is “Gird me, O Lord, with the cincture of purity, and quench in my heart the fire of concupiscence, that the virtue of continence and chastity may remain in me.”

The *Maniple* is a short narrow strip of cloth that hand from the left arm and represents the bands with which Jesus’ hands were tied. The vesting prayer is “Let me deserve, O Lord, to bear the maniple of tears and sorrow, so that one day I may come with joy into the reward of my labors.

The *Stole* is a long silk band that fits around the neck of the priest and is crossed on the breast of him and represents the rope that was tied around the neck of Jesus with which He was dragged from place to place. It is the symbol of authority in the Church. As a sign of his full priestly powers the bishop does not cross the stole in front. Only the Pope has the right to wear it always. The vesting prayer is “Restore to me, O Lord, the state of immortality which was lost to me by my first parents, and although unworthy to approach Thy sacred mysteries, grant me nevertheless eternal joy.

The *Chasuble* is the uppermost vestment worn by the priest at Mass and represents the purple robe put on Jesus to mock Him. It hangs from the shoulders, in front and behind, down almost to the knees. The vesting prayer is “O Lord, Who hast said ‘My yoke is sweet and my burden light,’ grant that I may carry it so as to obtain Thy grace.”

QUO PRIMUM (Apostolic Constitution)
From the very first, upon Our elevation to the chief Apostleship, We gladly turned our mind and energies and directed all out thoughts to those matters which concerned the preservation of a pure liturgy, and We strove with God's help, by every means in our power, to accomplish this purpose. For, besides other decrees of the sacred Council of Trent, there were stipulations for Us to revise and re-edit the sacred books: the Catechism, the Missal and the Breviary. With the Catechism published for the instruction of the faithful, by God's help, and the Breviary thoroughly revised for the worthy praise of God, in order that the Missal and Breviary may be in perfect harmony, as fitting and proper—for its most becoming that there be in the Church only one appropriate manner of reciting the Psalms and only one rite for the celebration of Mass—We deemed it necessary to give our immediate attention to what still remained to be done, viz, the re-editing of the Missal as soon as possible.

Hence, We decided to entrust this work to learned men of our selection. They very carefully collated all their work with the ancient codices in Our Vatican Library and with reliable, preserved or emended codices from elsewhere. Besides this, these men consulted the works of ancient and approved authors concerning the same sacred rites; and thus they have restored the Missal itself to the original form and rite of the holy Fathers. When this work has been gone over numerous times and further emended, after serious study and reflection, We commanded that the finished product be printed and published soon as possible, so that all might enjoy the fruits of this labor; and thus, priests would know which prayers to use and which rites and ceremonies they were required to observe from now on in the celebration of Masses.

Let all everywhere adopt and observe what has been handed down by the Holy Roman Church, the Mother and Teacher of the other churches, and let Masses not be sung or read according to any other formula than that of this Missal published by Us. This ordinance applies henceforth, now, and forever, throughout all the provinces of the Christian world, to all patriarchs, cathedral churches, collegiate and parish churches, be they secular or religious, both of men and of women—even of military orders—and of churches or chapels without a specific congregation in which conventual Masses are sung aloud in choir or read privately in accord with the rites and customs of the Roman Church. This Missal is to be used by all churches, even by those which in their authorization are made exempt, whether by Apostolic indult, custom, or privilege, or even if by oath or official confirmation of the Holy See, or have their rights and faculties guaranteed to them by any other manner whatsoever.

This new rite alone is to be used unless approval of the practice of saying Mass differently was given at the very time of the institution and confirmation of the church by Apostolic See at least 200 years ago, or unless there has prevailed a custom of a similar kind which has been continuously followed for a period of not less than 200 years, in which most cases We in no wise rescind their above-mentioned prerogative or custom. However, if this Missal, which we have seen fit to publish, be more agreeable to these latter, We grant them permission to celebrate Mass according to its rite, provided they have the consent of their bishop or prelate or of their whole Chapter, everything else to the contrary notwithstanding.

All other of the churches referred to above, however, are hereby denied the use of other missals, which are to be discontinued entirely and absolutely; whereas, by this present Constitution, which will be valid henceforth, now, and forever, We order and enjoin that nothing must be added to Our recently published Missal, nothing omitted from it, nor anything whatsoever be changed within it under the penalty of Our displeasure.

We specifically command each and every patriarch, administrator, and all other persons or whatever ecclesiastical dignity they may be, be they even cardinals of the Holy Roman Church, or possessed of any other rank or pre-eminence, and We order them in virtue of holy obedience to chant or to read the Mass according to the rite and manner and norm herewith laid down by

Us and, hereafter, to discontinue and completely discard all other rubrics and rites of other missals, however ancient, which they have customarily followed; and they must not in celebrating Mass presume to introduce any ceremonies or recite any prayers other than those contained in this Missal.

Furthermore, by these presents [this law], in virtue of Our Apostolic authority, We grant and concede in perpetuity that, for the chanting or reading of the Mass in any church whatsoever, this Missal is hereafter to be followed absolutely, without any scruple of conscience or fear of incurring any penalty, judgment, or censure, and may freely and lawfully be used. Nor are superiors, administrators, canons, chaplains, and other secular priests, or religious, of whatever title designated, obliged to celebrate the Mass otherwise than as enjoined by Us. We likewise declare and ordain that no one whosoever is as forced or coerced to alter this Missal, and that this present document cannot be revoked or modified, but remain always valid and retain its full force—notwithstanding the previous constitutions and decrees of the Holy See, as well as any general or special constitution or edicts of provincial or synodal councils, and notwithstanding the practice and custom of the aforesaid churches, established by long and immemorial prescription—except, however, if more than two hundred years' standing.

It is Our will, therefore, and by the same authority, We decree that, after We publish this constitution and the edition of the Missal, the priests of the Roman Curia are, after thirty days, obliged to chant or read the Mass according to it; all others south of the Alps, after three months; and those beyond the Alps either within six months or whenever the Missal is available for sale. Wherefore, in order that the Missal be preserved incorrupt throughout the whole world and kept free of flaws and errors, the penalty for nonobservance for printers, whether mediately or immediately subject to Our dominion, and that of the Holy Roman Church, will be the forfeiting of their books and a fine of one hundred gold ducats, payable ipso facto to the Apostolic Treasury. Further, as for those located in other parts of the world, the penalty is excommunication latae sententiae, and such other penalties as may in Our judgment be imposed; and We decree by this law that they must not dare or presume either to print or to publish or to sell, or in any way to accept books of this nature without Our approval and consent, or without the express consent of the Apostolic Commissaries of those places, who will be appointed by Us. Said printer must receive a standard Missal and agree faithfully with it and in no wise vary from the Roman Missal of the large type (secundum magnum impressionem).

Accordingly, since it would be difficult for this present pronouncement to be sent to all parts of the Christian world and simultaneously come to light everywhere, We direct that it be, as usual, posted and published at the doors of the Basilica of the Prince of the Apostles, also at the Apostolic Chancery, and on the street at Campo Flora; furthermore, We direct that printed copies of this same edict signed by a notary public and made official by an ecclesiastical dignitary possess the same indubitable validity everywhere and in every nation, as if Our manuscript were shown there. Therefore, no one whosoever is permitted to alter this notice of Our permission, statute, ordinance, command, precept, grant, indult, declaration, will, decree, and prohibition. Should know that he will incur the wrath of Almighty God and of the Blessed Apostles Peter and Paul.

Given at St. Peter's in the year of the Lord's Incarnation, 1570, on the 14th of July of the Fifth year of Our Pontificate.
H. Cumin. Ceasar Glorierius

VALUE OF HOLY MASS

At the hour of death the holy Masses you have heard devoutly will be your greatest consolation.

Every Mass will go with you to Judgment and will plead for pardon for you.

By every Mass you can diminish the temporal punishment due to your sins, more or less, according to your fervor.

By devoutly assisting at Holy Mass you render the greatest homage possible to the Sacred Humanity of Our Lord.

Through the Holy Sacrifice, Our Lord Jesus Christ supplies for many of your negligence's and omissions.

He forgives you all the venial sins which you are determined to avoid.

He forgives you all your unknown sins which you never confessed. The power of Satan over you is diminished.

By piously hearing Holy Mass you afford the Souls in Purgatory the greatest possible relief.

One Holy Mass heard during your life will be of more benefit to you than many heard for you after your death.

Catholic Apologetics: A look at some common thoughts about the Bible Alone.

Table of contents

FOR CATHOLICS

Dear Catholic reader, this section is dedicated to you and I offer the Body of Christ to you. For it is the Body of Christ that was sacrificed for you so that you may preserve in your faith and be strengthen against sin.

From the moment we are baptized we received a commission from Christ to go forth, teach the world and bring all to the true faith. Many of you have done so while others have no idea where to begin nor even know their own faith and cannot even do simple apologetics.

For those who have tried to teach the world you understand how often difficult it is to have Protestants and others understand even basic concepts of the Church. Often they will quote the bible, interpret it to their own meaning and expect you to believe as they do. Yet, at the same time if you use their own interpretations and strictly apply it to other sections, of the bible, they will say you are wrong and they are still right.

How frustrating is it to see our misguided brethren quote one section of the bible and yet completely ignore other sections simply because they either don't know it or it contradicts what they are trying to prove. When you point out this oversight they simply explain it away by saying something like, "I see your point, but….".

Some of you may think this book is below you because you are doing what Christ wanted. Therefore, I say to you that everyone cannot know everything and it is only by constant study and prayer that you can continue in your efforts. While many writers often cover the same subjects one can always learn something new about information they already know.

For those who lack understanding of the faith do not despair for there is still time.

Remember every Catholic started out with limited knowledge of the faith. Start today and begin reading books of the faith and soon you too will have knowledge to go forth with confidence and teach the world.

Pray today to the Holy Ghost and Our Mother for help in knowing the faith and the confidence to do what Christ wants you to do.

Remember, whatever you do for God and His Church He will reward you for it.

Daily Thought

The duty of every Catholic is to unquestionably and religiously fulfill, firmly safeguard and profess without timidity, both in private and in public live, the principals of Christian truths taught by the Magisterium of the Catholic Church...error is approved by non-resistance, and truth is suffocated by not defending Her.

-Pope St. Pius X

FOR PROTESTANTS

Dear Protestant reader, this section is dedicated to you and I offer to you the Precious Blood of Christ with which washed away the sins of the world. For it is with this Blood that many have been redeemed and saved from eternal damnation. This is the Blood that Christ was willing shed so that the gates of Heaven would be re-opened and that the elect allowed to enter.

You have received this book because someone cares about you. I assure you that I was once a member of your ranks. Even my ancestors changed from Catholic to Protestant over 400 years ago and I can say that for many generations, on my side of the family, there has never been a Catholic. I grew up in a Protestant church and then after events in my adult life I began a search for the true church of Christ. It was only after much thought, readings, prayer and searching for the truth that I was convinced that the Catholic Church is indeed the Church of Christ as much as the centurion was convinced that Christ was the Son of God (Mark 15:39).

Many of you who will read this will say "But I'm not a Protestant because I don't protest against the Catholic Church." Here you are in error because the *Dictionary of World Religions* states that a Protestant is "That form of Western Christianity which does not accept the authority of the pope…". If you are in error here where else might you error in your faith?

For those who protest against the Catholic Church saying it's not a true faith then think about your own faith. If Christ only founded one faith then what makes your beliefs better than the other faiths? And why do you interpret the Bible according to your own choosing instead of having a one and unifying belief?

Do not think that I have high hopes and can convert you with this book for faith is a gift from God. Also, do not think that I can answer every question and objection that you find; for there are many who are wiser than I. Remember, it is only God who can enlighten those who seek the truth.

It is only enough that I write what is in my heart and offer you encouragement as you seek the truth. Why should you not agree with me if you think I am correct?

First thoughts

Greetings reader! Chances are that this is the first time that we have crossed paths, even a spiritual one, on our roads towards truth and salvation. In honor of this occasion please sit awhile as I tell to you my tale. I offer to you a candle, to light your way, and a compass to point you in the right direction. For all you have to do is to look beyond this intersection and see the darkness and deceit that awaits you if you should ever stray off this path.

The idea for this section came about for many reasons. The most important of these are after close contacts with a Protestant group whom I found swept up in the ideas of private interpretation of the Bible and the belief that they are part of the true church of Christ. Often when I show them that their interpretations are wrong and what the correct ones are they defend their beliefs saying something like “the Holy Ghost inspires me therefore how can I be wrong?”

It is my experience that they, like many other religions, will only token listen to what the Church has been teaching for the past 2000 years.

If you may be wondering why I, a Catholic, have such a close contact with this group I will say that if we have met before then I need not explain further; and if this is our first meeting then suffice it to say that God has His reasons for leading me to them and having a discourse with them.

But these contacts have not been without problems. For I have had many friends depart from me and will never more will walk again with me. To them my prayers go forth as they continue on a different route than the one I have taken. In the end it is better for them to depart than for me to depart from this path of faith.

Another reason is that I have had several e-mails from Protestants who argue against the Catholic Church. Here, they try to interpret the Bible one way and want me to agree with them. However, when I use their beliefs against them and do strict interpretations showing why they are wrong or how the Bible could be interpreted another way they often get angry and usually are never heard from them again.

In this book we will look at certain quotes from scripture, show how they should be strictly interpreted, then give some ideas on why it is wrong and what the Catholic Church has to say about the topic.

All quotes from the Bible are taken from the Douay-Rheims version. This section is dedicated to the ending of the Waldensian heresy that still exists and to St. Dominic who led many of them back to the faith; may he also led those who are seeking to know the truth to the Catholic faith. Finally, to Reverend Mother Marie De Montfort, for many reasons that I am sure God will reward her for in Eternity

CHURCH FOUNDATIONS

And I say to thee: That thou are Peter; and upon this rock I will build my church, and the gates of hell shall not prevail against it (Matthew 16:18)

Interpretation

We can see that only Christ will construct a church because He uses the word "my" and not "us" or "our". Because Christ is a son of a carpenter we know that He will have the skills and tools to build any type of structure He wants.

Here Christ is showing Peter which particular rock He will build upon and has declared the name of His church as "my church."

Therefore, the only true church is the one that Christ built and the religion He founded is called "my" and not Christian, Protestant, Catholic or some other given name.

Consider this

* Christ founded a church which was to continue forever until the end of time. While it is true that Christ never gave a proper name to His church He did leave it with four marks, or identifiers, that everyone could recognize. These marks are one, holy, universal and apostolic.

* The Church is one can be proven by Paul who wrote "One body and one Spirit…One Lord, one faith, one baptism"

(Ephesians 4:4-5). For the Church needs to have the same teaching, the same laws, the same Sacraments and the same form of worship.

Since the time of Christ there have been about 30,000 different Protestant groups (this means that a new group appears about once every 3-4 weeks) and each one has a different believe and laws from the other groups.

* The Church is holy can be demonstrated in Ephesians 5:25-27 which says "Christ also loved the Church and delivered Himself up for it…not having spot or wrinkle…but …holy and without blemish." Since Christ was holy He would only found a church that teaches holy doctrine and gives its members what is needed to lead a holy life no matter their station or when they live.

* The Church is universal can be shown from Matthew 28:19 which states: "Going, therefore, teach ye all nations." Christ gave the commandment to teach all nations and not just a few. The Church of Christ has to be located and taught in all nations.

* The Church is apostolic can be proven from the end of Matthew 28:19-20 which continues: "And behold I am with you all days, even to the consummation of the world." Christ knew He was going to leave the world soon and knew that His Apostles would not live forever. Therefore, the Apostles would teach and instruct others ("And when they had ordained to them priests in every * The Church is one can be proven by St. Paul who wrote "One body and one Spirit…One Lord, one faith, one baptism" (Ephesians 4:4-5). For the Church needs to have the same teaching, the same laws, the same Sacraments and the same form of worship.

* Finally, think of the Church which has been persecuted the greatest number of times, and has survived and that has performed the greatest number of miracles. For Christ said "Remember my word that I said to you: The servant is not greater than his master. If they have persecuted me, they will also persecute you…the hour cometh, that whosoever killeth you, will think that he doth a service to God" (John 15:20, 16:2). What church has suffered much in attacks, both physical and written/oral, and has maintained itself even if it is smaller before the attacks began and then grew once the attacks were over?

* For miracles look at His Church that has made the lame walk, the blind see, the deaf to hear again and the dead raised from their eternal sleep. For did not Christ say: "Believe you not that I am in the Father, and the Father in me? Otherwise believe for the very works' sake. Amen, amen I say to you, he that believeth in me, the works that I do, he also shall do; and greater than these shall he do" (John 14:11-12). If Christ performed many miracles then why should many who followed later not be able to do the same things?

The Church Teaches

Letter of the Holy Office to the Bishop of England, 1864

The true Church of Jesus Christ is constituted by divine authority and is known by four notes. We lay down these notes as matters of faith in the Creed. And any one of these notes is so joined to the others that it cannot be separated from them. Hence it is that the Church is really catholic, and is called Catholic, must, at the same time, shine with the prerogatives of unity, sanctity and apostolic succession. Therefore, the Catholic Church is one by conspicuous and perfect unity of the whole world and of all peoples, by that unity, indeed, whose principles, root and never failing source is the supreme authority and "greater sovereignty" of St. Peter, the Prince of the Apostles, and of his successors in the Roman Chair. Nor is any other church catholic except that which has been built upon Peter alone and which rises into one body closely joined and knit together in the unity of faith and love."

Thoughts to Ponder

"Christianity is the great Church and nothing else is Christianity. To call anything else Christianity is to plunge into confusion and chaos; and it is an insult to Christianity. Christianity is a great thing, not a little one; one thing, not many things; a rich thing, not a poor thing; a majestic thing, not a thing of shreds and patches. Christianity is Christianity at its noblest, truest and more comprehensive, and that is the Catholic Church. If you desire to be a Christian, join it. It will make no demands upon you that are more fearful than the demands made upon you by any peddling form of Christianity. It asks no greater sacrifice than Little Bethel or the Church of England; and it does not insult your intelligence by inviting you to become a member of a contradiction in terms."
-Professor J. Middleton Murray, a non-Catholic critic

"She is called catholic by all her enemies, as well as by her own children. Heretics and schismatics can call the Church by no other name than catholic; for they would not be understood, unless they use the name by which the Church is known to the whole world."- St. Cyril

"As I have already observed, the Church having received this preaching and this faith, although scattered throughout the world, yet as if occupying one house, carefully preserves it…For the churches which have been planted in Germany do not believe or hand down anything different, nor do those in Spain, nor do those in Gaul, nor do those in the East, nor do those in Egypt, nor do those in Libya, nor do those which have been established in the central regions of the world." –St. Irenaeus

"The nations of the earth pass away, and the thrones fall to the ground, the Church alone remains."- Napoleon Bonaparte

CHURCH LEADERSHIP

And I will give to thee the keys of the kingdom of heaven. And whatsoever thou shalt bind upon earth, it shall be bound also in heaven: and whatsoever thou shalt loose on earth, it shall be loosed also in heaven. (Matthew 16:19)

Interpretation

Christ physically gave Peter the only set of keys to Heaven. Therefore, those jokes about Peter guarding the gates of Heaven are true because only Peter has the keys and if he ever loses them then perhaps the gates will either be forever opened or closed depending on his last action at the gates. (One could only wonder why Peter wasn't trained as a locksmith just in case the keys ever got lost and the gates were locked.)

Whatever Peter alone shall bind or loosen on earth Heaven will also imitate. Therefore, since Peter was a fisherman by trade he could bind a group of fish and Heaven would imitate it.

Consider this

* In John 21:15-17 Christ asks St. Peter to feed his lambs. We know that Christ didn't have an actually group of sheep but that he was speaking about His followers and that St. Peter was to be the leader of them. To no one else did Christ give this commandment.

* In Matthew 16:16 Peter responses to Christ's question about who did they think He was by saying "…Thou art Christ, the Son of the living God." To which Christ singled out Peter by changing his name, giving him the keys (which in ancient times was a symbol of jurisdiction) to Heaven and saying that whatever St. Peter shall bind or loosen on earth will be copied in Heaven. Christ also said this to no other of his followers.

Proofs of the leadership of St. Peter are as followed: It was St. Peter who proposed the election of another to take the place of Judas (Acts 1:15-26). It was Peter who preached the first sermon on the day of Pentecost (Acts 2:14-41). It was Peter that admitted the first convert from Judaism (Acts 2:38-41) and paganism (Acts 10). It was Peter who worked the first miracle after the ascension of Christ (Acts 3:6-8). It was St. Peter who gave out the first punishment (Acts 5:1-10). In the first Council at Jerusalem, there was much disputing but when St. Peter spoke all submitted (Acts 15:7-12). Finally, after his conversion St. Paul presented himself to St. Peter (Galatians 1:18)

Some will claim that at the meeting in Jerusalem it was St. James who spoke the final words. While this is true all St. James did was to paraphrase St. Peter's words by saying "Simon hath related how God first visited to take of the Gentiles a people to his name" (Acts 15:14).

* More proof of St. Peter's lead position can be gathered from looking at who is always listed first among the Apostles; St. Peter is always listed first and Judas is always listed last. St. Peter's name is listed 179 times while John, the second most listed, is only mentioned 30 times. In fact the total number of times the Apostles are mentioned, minus St. Peter, is 149.

The Church Teaches

-

From *The Establishment of the Apostolic Primacy in St. Peter,* *Vatican Council, 1869-70*

We teach and declare, therefore, according to the testimony of the Gospel that the primacy of jurisdiction over the whole Church of God was immediately and directly promised to and conferred upon the blessed Apostle Peter by Christ the Lord. For to Simon, Christ said, "Thou shalt be called Cephas". Then, after Simon had acknowledged Christ with the confession, "Thou are the Christ, the Son of the living God", it was to Simon alone that the solemn words were spoken by the Lord: "Blessed art thou, Simon Bar-Jona, for flesh and blood has not revealed this to thee, but my Father in heaven. And I say to thee, thou art Peter, and upon this rock I will build my Church, and they gates of hell shall not prevail against it. And I will give thee the keys of the kingdom of heaven; and whatever thou shalt bind on earth shall be bound in heaven, and whatever thou shalt loose on earth shall be loosed in heaven". And after his Resurrection, Jesus conferred upon Simon Peter alone the jurisdiction of supreme shepherd and ruler over his whole flock with the words, "Feed my lambs…Feed my sheep". In open opposition to this very clear teaching of the Holy Scriptures, as it has always been understood by the Catholic Church, are the perverse opinions of those who wrongly explain the form of government established by Christ in his Church; either by denying the Peter alone in preference to the other apostles, either singly or as a group, was endowed by Christ with the true and proper primacy of jurisdiction; or by claiming that this same primacy was not given immediately and directly to St. Peter, but to the Church and through the Church to Peter as an agent of the Church.

Thoughts to Ponder

"All attempts to explain the "Rock" in any other way than referring to Peter have ignominiously failed. Neither the confession of Peter nor the faith of Peter is an adequate explanation." -Plummer, an Anglican exegete

"In spite of all Protestant attempts to weaken its force, it cannot be doubted that this passage [Matthew 16:16] contains the solemn proclamation of the primacy of Peter. He is declared to be the founder of the Church, the bearer of the keys and the sovereign lawgiver, whose precepts and prohibitions have the force of divinely sanctioned laws." -Professor Otto Pfleiderer, from the non-Catholic Tubingen School

PRIESTHOOD

And call none your father upon earth; for one is your father, who is in heaven. (Matthew 23:9)

Interpretation

This is a clear call to erase the usage of the word "father" from all context and meaning. The only person who could be called "father" is God Himself. Therefore, anyone, on earth, who calls himself "father" is declaring himself God.

Consider this

* In Matthew 23:10 Christ says to call none "masters" or teachers. Therefore, should we also outlaw the use of this word as well. Why isn't there an uproar in using the word "master" or "teacher"? The Bible forbids us to give anyone the respect and honor due to God the Father.

* If we cannot use the word "father" then what shall we call the male biological parent of children? No one has ever called for the elimination of the word "father" when dealing with the male parent of a child. If we are forbidden to use the word "father" then wouldn't this be considered a sin against God?

* In 1 Corinthians 4:15-16 St. Paul writes "… for in Christ Jesus, by the gospel I have begotten you. Wherefore I beseech you, be ye followers of me, as I also am of Christ." Here St. Paul is calling himself a "father" of many people and telling them that they should follow his example.

*It has been argued that all are part of a universal priesthood based upon 1 Peter 2:9: "You are a chosen race, a royal priesthood, a holy nation." While it is true that all offer up a spiritual sacrifice it is only the Apostles, and their successors, who can offer up a true sacrifice to God.

* The priesthood was established by God Himself in the Old Testament. It was restricted to the tribe of Levi and only the first-born of the house of Aaron could enter the Holy of Holies and offer sacrifice for the whole nation. In the New Testament Christ kept the institution of priesthood and conferred it upon a select group of men with one being chosen as their leader.

* In the book of Acts it is made clear that only a few, not everyone, were ordained as priests to lead the faithful.

The Church Teaches

from The Council of Trent, 1545-63

In conformity with God's decree, sacrifice and priesthood are so related that both exist in every law. Therefore, in the New Testament, since the Catholic Church has received the holy and visible sacrifice of the Eucharist according to the institution of the Lord, it is likewise necessary to acknowledge that there is in the Church a new, visible, and external priesthood, into which the old priesthood was changed. Moreover, Sacred Scripture makes it clear and the tradition of the Catholic Church has always taught that this priesthood was instituted by the same Lord our Savior, and that the power of consecration, offering, and administering his body and blood, and likewise the power of remitting and of retaining sins, was given to the apostles and to their successors in the priesthood.

Thoughts to Ponder

Once a Protestant minister went to hear a priest in France at the cathedral of Notre Dame. The priest came out and gave the sign of the cross with such holy and majestic movement that the minister told his companions: "He has already preached to us: the sermon is over, we can go." - taken from the life of Fr. Ravignan

BIBLE ALONE

And because from they infancy thou hast known the holy scriptures, which can instruct thee to salvation, by the faith which is Christ Jesus. All scripture, inspired of God, is profitable to teach, to reprove, to correct, to instruct in justice. (2 Timothy 3:16)

Interpretation

Because the New Testament had not been put together the only books of the Bible we can use are the Old Testament because these are the books that Timothy would have learned at a young age. For did not Christ Himself say "Do not think that I am come to destroy the law, or the prophets. I am not come to destroy, but to fulfill" (Matthew 5:17). Let us now throw away the books of the New Testament and read only those scriptures of the Old.

Consider this

* Nowhere in the Bible does Christ command his followers to write anything. In fact, He tells them "Going therefore, teach ye all nations…Teaching them to observe all things whatsoever I have commanded you…." (Matthew 28:19-20). Christ commanded a teaching church and not a book writing church. Nor did Christ say that they could interpret what Christ taught them.

* St. Paul wrote "Therefore, brethren, stand fast; and hold the traditions which you have learned, whether by word, or by our epistle" (2 Thessalonians 2:14) because not everything that Christ said or did is written in the Bible (John 21:25). Oral tradition is just as important as the written word. It is by tradition that we honor God on Sunday instead of Saturday.

*It is often claimed that what was not written, in the Bible, is not important. My questions are: 'How can you be sure?' and 'What is your scriptural proof for this?' For there are many books that the Bible mentions and yet are not included. Should it not be that if they were important to mention then they should be just as important to be included? How can one be sure that the mentioned books don't contain something that is important for faith?

* Because the last book of the New Testament was finished about 65 years after the Ascension of Christ the question that must be asked is "Who or what served as the final authority during this time?" Also, it wasn't until the end of the 4th Century that the first definitive list of books was created. Therefore, how did the early Christians know what books to read?

* The idea of the Bible alone didn't exist until the 14th Century when John Wycliffe started teaching this doctrine.

* It wasn't until the invention of the printing press that the Bible could be mass-produced and given to everyone. However, most of the people couldn't read or write so how did they read or learn the Bible? In fact, during the time of the destruction of

Jerusalem it has been estimated that only 3 percent of the population of Israel could read and write. While the estimation can be disputed one can see that in many societies that basically those working for the government or with religion would be able to need to read and write. As you move away from learning centers and cities the less likely you would find someone who is able to read and write.

* Not everyone can interpret scripture for it was St. Peter who was alarmed at this practice and warned that there "are certain things hard to understand, which the unlearned and unstable wrest, as they do also the other scriptures, to their own destruction." (2 Peter 3:16)

The Bible needs an official teacher. It was the Ethiopian who answered St. Philip, when questioned about if he understood what he was reading, "And how can I, unless some man shew me…" (Acts 8:31)? Without the writers themselves to show us what they meant it is from tradition and teaching of the Church that the true meanings are found.

* It is tradition that teaches us to go and worship God on Sundays, to celebrate the birth of Christ on December 25 and that there are certain books that make up the Bible.

The Church Teaches

from The Council of Trent, 1543-63

The holy, ecumenical, and general Council of Trent, which has lawfully assembled in the Holy Spirit and is presided over by the same three legates of the Apostolic See, has always as its purpose to remove error and preserve in the Church the purity of the gospel that was originally promised by the prophets in Sacred Scripture and first promulgated by the Son of God himself, our Lord Jesus Christ. He, in turn, ordered his apostles, who are the source of all saving truth and moral teaching, to preach it to every creature. The council is aware that this truth and teaching are contained in the written books and in the unwritten traditions that the apostles received from Christ himself or that were handed on, as it were from hand to hand, from the apostles under the inspiration of the Holy Spirit, and so have come down to us. The council follows the example of the orthodox Fathers and the same sense of devotion and reverence with which it accepts and venerates all the books of both the Old and the New Testament, since one God is the author of both, it also accepts and venerated traditions concerned with faith and morals as having been received orally from Christ or inspired by the Holy Spirit and continuously preserved in the Catholic Church. It judged, however, that a list of the Sacred Books should be written into this decree so that no one may doubt which books the council accepts. The list is as follows.

The Old Testament: five books of Moses, that is, Genesis, Exodus, Leviticus, Numbers, Deuteronomy; Josue, Judges, Ruth, four book of Kings, two of Paralipomenon; the first book of Esdras and the second, which is called Nehemias; Tobis, Judith, Esther, Job, David's Psalter of one hundred and fifty psalms, Proverbs, Ecclesiastes, the Canticle of Canticles, Wisdom, Ecclesiasticus, Isaias, Jeremias with Baruch, Ezechiel, Daniel; the twelve minor prophets, that is, Osee, Joel, Amos, Abdias, Jonas, Micheas, Nahum, Habacuc, Sophonias, Aggeus, Zacharias, Malachias; two books of Macabees, the first and the second.

The New Testament: the four Gospels, according to Matthew, Mark, Luke, and John; the Acts of the Apostles, written by the Evangelist Luke, fourteen epistles of the Apostle Paul: to the Romans two to the Corinthians, to the Galatians, to the Ephesians, to the Philippians, to the Colossians, two to the Thessalonians, two to Timothy, to Titus, to Philemon, to the Hebrews; two epistles of the Apostle Peter, three of the Apostle John, one of the Apostle James, one of the Apostle Jude; and the Apocalypse of the Apostle John. Moreover, if anyone does not accept these books as sacred and canonical in their entirety, with all their parts, according to the text usually read in the Catholic Church as they are in the ancient Latin Vulgate, but knowingly and willfully contemns the traditions previously mentioned: let him be anathema...

Thoughts to Ponder

"Men willingly believe what they wish."

-Julius Caesar, *De Bello Gallico*

"It is absolutely wrong and it is forbidden either to narrow inspiration to certain parts only of the Scripture, or to admit that the sacred writer has erred…The system of those who limit divine inspiration to matters of faith and morals cannot be tolerated"

- Pope Leo XIII, *Providentissimus Deus*

"What else gives rise to so many heresies except that the Scripture, which is excellent in itself, is falsely understood?" - St. Augustine

SALVATION

For God so loved the world, as to give his only begotten Son; that whosoever believeth in him, may not perish, but may have life everlasting. (John 3:16)

Interpretation

As long as I believe in God I can do anything that I want. Therefore, crimes such as adultery and murder I can perform as long as I believe. I also do not have to be baptized nor attend any church or religion. After all, I believe in God and that is all that is required of me.

Consider this

* Having a belief is a good first step. However, only believing isn't good enough for God. For example, I can firmly believe that this paper you are reading is really a winning lottery ticket; but no matter how hard I believe that this is a lottery ticket doesn't make it one.

* Besides believing you must have faith. "But without faith it is impossible to please God. For he that cometh to God, must believe that he is, and is a rewarder to them that seek him" (Hebrews 11:6) and "For by grace you are saved through faith, and that not of yourselves, for it is the gift of God" (Ephesians 2:8).

* For faith to be rewarded it must be active and alive. "For even as the body without spirit is dead; so also faith without works is dead." (James 2:26). Chief among the works of good are: To feed the hungry, To give drink to the thirsty, To clothe the naked, To visit the imprisoned, To shelter the homeless, To visit the sick, To bury the dead, To admonish the sinner, To instruct the ignorant, To counsel the doubtful, To comfort the sorrowful, To bear wrongs patiently, To forgive all injuries, To pray for the living and the dead.

* Even with faith salvation is not assured. "And if the just man shall scarcely be saved, where shall the ungodly and the sinner appear" (1 Peter 4:18)? To think yourself as just or saved is folly "for all have sinned, and do need the glory of God" (Romans 3:23). Even Christ said "For the Son of Man shall come in the glory of his Father with his angels and then will be render to every man according to his works." (Matthew 16:27).

* Everyone is not saved. Christ spoke "Not everyone that saith to me, Lord, Lord, shall enter into the kingdom of heaven: but he that doth the will of my Father who is in heaven, he shall enter into the kingdom of heaven." (Matthew 7:21). Also, at the Last Supper Christ said "For this is my blood of the new testament, which shall be shed for many unto remission of sins." (Matthew 26:28). Here many might claim that Christ really said "shall be shed for all" and not "for many." This is disproved in Luke 2:34 when Simeon says "Behold this child is set for the fall, and for the resurrection of many in Israel…". Notice that he said the "resurrection of many" and not the "resurrection of all."

* While it is indeed true that Christ shed his blood for the salvation of all one needs only to look at the fruits of it we can see that it only applies to many of mankind and not all of it. For when Christ said "for you" He meant those that were His disciples and when He said "for many" He meant the remainder of the elect. "For many are called, but few are chosen" (Matthew 22:14)

* In order for a chance at salvation one must do penance. "But unless you shall do penance, you shall all likewise perish" (Luke 13: 3). For upon death we will all be judged according to our own works. "Therefore I will judge every many according to his ways, O house of Israel, saith the Lord God. Be converted, and do penance for all your iniquities: and iniquity shall not be your ruin" (Ezechiel 18:30).

* Since we are to be judged according to our sins we must do penance and good works because "charity coverth a multitude of sins" (1 Peter 4:8). But yet it does not cover all sins. Therefore, we must confess our sins because "he that hideth his sins shall not prosper; but he that shall confess and forsake them shall obtain mercy." (Proverbs 28:13).

* Many will say that we should confess only to God. While it is true that God may forgive your sins there is no assurance that He will. Other will say that we need to "confess therefore your sins to one another; and pray for each other, that you may be saved. For the continual prayer of a just man availeth much." (James 5:16). The question is: when did the person sitting next to you receive the power to forgive sins? For only God can forgive sins (Luke 5:24-25).

* Christ gave the power to forgive sins to the Apostles and their successors. He told the Apostles "whose sins you shall forgive, they are forgiven them: and whose sins you shall retain, they are retained" (John 20:23). We know that when we confess our sins to a successor of the Apostles we know that if they forgive our sins than God will also forgive our sins.

In Acts 6:1-7 the Apostles told the people to choose seven men so they could carry on with the preaching and teaching of Christ. It was only these men whom the Apostles laid hand upon and gave them the power of the priesthood. Not all received the power of ministry. For in 2 Corinthians 5:18-19 Paul writes "But all things are of God, who hath reconciled us to himself by Christ; and hath given to us the ministry of reconciliation. For God indeed was in Christ, reconciling the world to himself; and he hath placed in us the word of reconciliation."

* Remember "that penance and remission of sins should be preached in his name, unto all nations, beginning at Jerusalem" (Luke 24: 47). Since sin weakens and kills the soul it is only by doing penance and confession that we may be pleasing to God; for as a child of God we may be like the prodigal son who left his father and upon his return his father said to him "Because this my son was dead and is come to life again, was lost and is found" (Luke 15:24). Also, "there shall be joy in heaven upon one sinner that doth penance, more than upon ninety-nine just who need not penance" (Luke 15:7).

The Church Teaches

from the Council of Trent, 1545-63

If all the regenerated had enough gratitude to God to keep forever the justice received in baptism by his grace and goodness, there would have been no need to institute any other sacrament than baptism for the remission of sins. But since God is rich in mercy and knows our frail structure, he has also prepared a remedy of life for those who, after baptism, have given themselves over to the slavery of sin and to the power of the devil. This remedy is the sacrament of penance, and through it the benefit of Christ's death is applied to those who have fallen after baptism. At all times all men who were stained by mortal sin have needed penance to obtain grace and justice. It is equally necessary likewise for those who would ask to be purified by the sacrament of baptism so that they might cast off and correct their wickedness and show their detestation of so great an offense against God by their hatred of sin and by the true sorrow of their soul. Therefore the prophet says: "Be converted and do penance for all your iniquities: and iniquity shall not be your ruin." And our Lord also said: "Unless you repent, you will all perish in the same manner." And Peter, the Prince of the Apostles, likewise recommends penance to sinners who are preparing themselves for baptism, "Repent and be baptized every one of you." However, penance was not a sacrament before the coming of Christ, and even after his coming it is not a sacrament for anyone who has not

Thoughts to ponder

"As long as God was not made man, there was no strict command for man to confess his sins to man; but since God became man, He has given all judgment to His Son, for He is appointed judge of the living and the dead; and to Him, therefore, is man to render an account of his sins. But, because Christ has ascended to Heaven, He has delegated his priests to exercise that power, and He has declared in express terms that they have jurisdiction over sins to bind and to loose."

–St. Thomas of Villanova

"Let no one say to me I do penance in my heart, I confess all my sins to God and to God alone, who was present when I committed sin. It is He who must forgive me. Then in vain was it said to the apostles, 'Whose sins you shall forgive they are forgiven, and whose sins you shall retain they are retained!' Then the Church has received the keys to no purpose; and so you make a mockery of the Gospel."

–St Augustine

BAPTISM

Teach ye all nations baptizing them in the name of the Father and of the Son and of the Holy Ghost. (Matthew 8:18)

Interpretation

Since North and South America were not known at the time of Christ there is no known account of any of the Apostles going there. Therefore, no one from those regions can be baptized because there is no biblical proof of it. Furthermore, the only people that could be baptized are listed in Acts 2:9-11 and Acts 8:27-38. There is no other proof of other regions being baptized.

Consider this

* Christ founded a church for not only His present but the future as well. Therefore, it doesn't matter what areas were known and unknown during His time. For Christ commanded "Go ye into the whole world and preach the gospel to every creature. He that believeth and is baptized shall be saved: but he that believeth not shall be condemned" (Mark 16:15-16). The act of teaching all nations the Gospel of Christ and the saving of your soul are something that is commanded of all those who are baptized.

* Baptism is necessary to enter into Heaven. "Amen, amen, I say to thee unless a man be born again of water and the Holy Ghost, he cannot enter into the kingdom of God" (John 3:5). It does not matter what you believe or how much faith you have for without baptism you cannot enter Heaven and any of your good works and the death of Christ shall have been in vain.

* The effects of baptism makes us members of Christ's Church, children of God, heirs of heaven with the right to enter into Heaven if we are worthy and takes away original sin. This sin is called original because it was the first sin and because of it death came; "Wherefore as by one man sin entered into this world, and by sin death; and so death passed upon all men, in whom all have sinned" (Romans 5:12). We enter into this world with this sin but baptism takes away this sin and our soul is clean.

Because of the sin of Adam all mankind must suffer. For now we all must labor and die. We also have a lesser understanding of God than Adam did; because we don't have the same knowledge as to the nature and will of God we are subject to temptation and sin. In Romans 7:23 it is written "I see another law in my members, fighting against the law of my mind." Here the forces of good and evil battle for control and it is with baptism that help to control evil thoughts and actions for even with baptism we still must all labor and die.

If you should think that the sin of Adam should not fall upon those who came after him consider the example of a ruler who gave his favorite subject a piece of land for all time provided that he followed the ruler's laws. The subject broke some of the laws and was driven off the land never to return. Because of the fault of one man his descendents were also deprived of the land as well. This is how it is with Adam- because of one man we are not allowed the gifts and land that God gave him.

* There are two ways to be baptized with water. One is total immersion into water and the other is to have water poured onto the skin. While immersion was the preferred way of baptism it would be impossible for the Apostles to do so when, on the first few days of the Church, 8,000 people were baptized. Let's assume that on the day when 5,000 entered into the Church there was 84 male followers of Christ present (this is the 12 Apostles and the 72 followers; numbers can be debatable because there is no number given in the Bible). This would mean that each follower had to baptized about 60 people. Assuming that it would take 4 minutes (breaks included) from the time the person stepped into the water, questions about their sincerity of faith, became immersed, words of baptism said, stepped out and the next person arrived it would take each follower about 4 hours to baptized all. If there were only the 12 Apostles, and the above assumption made and each Apostle did 416 people, then it would take each about 28 hours.

Now assume the above conditions but with only the pouring of the water takes 3 minutes. It would take each follower about 3 hours. For with only the Apostles it would take about 21 hours.

* Also, there is nowhere in the Bible that shows exactly how a baptism was done; the most the Bible tells us is that people were baptized. Moreover, when Christ washed the feet of His disciples He said, "He that is washed needeth not but to wash his feet, but is clean wholly. And you are clean, but not all" (John 13:10). If Christ needed to only wash the feet of his disciples to make them clean then does one need to be fully immersed to be baptized?

* Many will say that infants are not to be baptized because Peter said, "Do penance, and be baptized everyone of you in the name of Jesus Christ, for the remission of your sins: and you shall received the gift of the Holy Ghost" (Acts 2:38). It is argued that infants cannot repent or do penance because they lack the intelligence to understand. If this is the case then perhaps we should withhold food, clothing and shelter from newborns because they don't understand either the meaning of this things. Additionally, since God gives each of us a guardian angel who is to say that our angel doesn't communicate with our soul and teaches us the glories of God. Further, we can tell that one of the first thing an infant learns is to recognize their mother and to understand the security of love that comes with it.

* Under the old law circumcision was the covenant between God and man. This was to be performed on all males of eight days old (Genesis 17:12) and there is nothing in the Bible about parents rejecting on the ground that the child wouldn't understand. Since baptism is the new covenant with God one can assume that infants would also be included.

* Nowhere in the Bible does Christ make mention of excluding infants from Baptism. While there is no mention specifically of infants being baptized the Bible tells of large groups and families being baptized. Common sense would be to say that infants were also included in these ceremonies.

Christ also called upon a child to sit upon him saying "…unless you be converted, and become as little children, you shall not enter the kingdom of heaven" (Matthew 18:2-4). He also rebuked his followers when they tried to stop children from coming to see Him and He said, "Suffer the little children, and forbid them not to come to me: for the kingdom of heaven is for such" (Matthew 19:13-15). If children were to be excluded from receiving baptism then why did Christ make them an example on how we are suppose to act?

* In the Roman catacombs there is proof of infant baptism: "Verina received [baptism] at the age of ten months, Florina at the age of twelve months", "Here rests Achillia, a new-baptized [infant]; she was one year and five months old, died February 23rd." Since these Christians lived closer to the time of Christ and His followers they would have a better understanding of what Christ taught. If they were wrong doing infant baptism then we are wrong today. If they were right in doing infant baptism then we are right today.

* St. Augustine and other early church fathers stated that infant baptism has been the practice of the church since its inception. Also, heresies of the faith have been confronted soon after their introduction. It wasn't until the 1520's that any serious challenges to infant baptism were given; therefore giving further proof that no error existed.

* Finally, tradition forces many Protestant faiths to admit the Catholic principal of tradition rather than surrender the practice of infant baptism.

The Church Teaches

from the Second Council of Orange, 529

If anyone asserts that Adam's sin was injurious only to Adam and not to his descendents, or if he declares that it was only the death of the body which is punishment for sin, and not the sin, the death of the soul, that passed from one man to all the human race, he attributes an injustice to God and contradicts the words of the Apostle: "Through one man sin entered into the world and through sin death, and thus death has passed into all men because all have sinned".

from a letter to the Archbishop of Arles, 1201

For they maintain that it is useless to confer baptism on infants...Our answer is that baptism has taken place of circumcision...Therefore, as the soul of the circumcised was not destroyed out of his people, so shall he who is born again of water and the Holy Spirit gain entrance into the kingdom of Heaven...Although original sin was remitted through the mystery of circumcision, and the danger of damnation averted, still no one entered the kingdom of heaven, for heaven was closed to everyone until the death of Christ. But through the sacrament of baptism made red with the blood of Christ, sin is remitted and entrance is gained to the kingdom of heaven; for Christ's blood has mercifully opened the door of heaven to his faithful. For it would not be fitting that all little children, so many of whom die each day, perish without having some remedy for salvation provided for them by the merciful God who wills that no one perish…The adversaries say that faith or charity and the other virtues are not infused in the children since children do not give consent; but the majority do not admit that statement in its absolute sense…Some assert that through the power of baptism the guilt in little children is taken away, but grace is not conferred upon them; others say that sin is forgiven and that virtues are infused, and that infants have the virtues as habits, but do not have the use of them until they become adults…We say that a distinction has to be made because there are two types of sin, namely, original and actual. Original sin is contracted without consent whereas actual sin is committed with consent. Therefore, original sin, which is contracted without consent, is forgiven without consent through the power of the sacrament; but actual sin, which is contracted with consent, is by no means forgiven without consent…The punishment for original sin is the loss of the vision of God; the punishment for actual sin is the torment of an everlasting hell.

Thoughts to ponder

"It is not enough merely to believe. He who believes and is not baptized, but is only a catechumen, had not yet fully acquired salvation." - St. Thomas Aquinas

St. Francis de Sales would often lead his young companions to the parish church, arrange them around the font where they had been baptized and say, "See, this is the spot that should be dearer to us than any other, for here it was we were made children of God." Then they would all give thanksgiving for God's mercy and disperse for their games.

HOLY EUCHARIST

Then Jesus said to them: Amen, amen I say unto you: Except you eat the flesh of the Son of man, and drink his blood, you shall not have life in you. He that eateth my flesh, and drinketh my blood, hath everlasting life: and I will raise him up in the last day. (John 6:54-55)

Interpretation

At this point the Apostles must have been a big disappointment to Christ. For here Christ commanded all to eat and drink His body and blood. Therefore, the Apostles should have done exactly what Christ commanded but, instead, nothing happened and Christ had to die on the cross instead of where He was standing at the time He spoke these words.

Consider this

* When Christ spoke the words in John 6:54-55 many of His followers left Him and followed no more (John 6:67). When they left Christ did not call them back nor did He say that He was speaking only in parables or that He was only trying to make a point with the Jewish people. While the Apostles did not fully understand these words they knew, in time, Christ would make it clear to them because Christ "hast the words of eternal life" (John 6:69).

* At the Last Supper Christ said, "This is my body" and "This is my blood" (Matthew 26:26-28). Here Christ did not say, "Pretend this is my body" or "Let's assume it's my body" or anything towards this nature; He said "This is…". When Christ spoke in parables the reader of the Bible is informed of this or Christ began to compare one thing to another. At the Last Supper there is no mention of a parable being spoken of nor does Christ compare the bread and wine to His body and blood.

* After changing the bread and wine into His body and blood Christ commanded the Apostles to "do this in commemoration of me" (Luke 22:19). This is to say that the Apostles, and their successors, must turn bread and wine into the body and blood of Christ. For without the power to do so then how would anyone be able to eat the body and blood of Christ which was commanded about a year before the Last Supper?

* In 1 Corinthians 10:16 St. Paul states "The chalice of benediction, which we bless, it is not the communion of the blood of Christ? And the bread, which we break, it is not the partaking of the body of the Lord." If the bread and wine did not change into the body and blood of Christ then wouldn't Paul have said that the bread and wine were symbols that represented them?

* Also, why would St. Paul say, "therefore whosoever shall eat this bread, or drink the chalice of the Lord unworthily, shall be guilty of the body and blood of the Lord" (1 Corinthians 11:27) if all a person was eating and drinking was just a piece of bread and some wine?

* It is often asked how can God be in so many pieces of bread. The answer is that God is almighty. Consider that God walked the face of the earth and at the same time was present in Heaven. It is God who commands and it is done; for it was God who created the universe, brought flood to the world, destroyed Sodom and Gomorrah, parted the Red Sea, cured the blind and deaf and changed water into wine. For with God all things are possible (Matthew 19:26).

The Church Teaches

from the Council of Trent, 1545-1563

To begin with, the holy council teaches and openly and straightforwardly professes that in the blessed sacrament of the Holy Eucharist, after the consecration of the bread and wine, our Lord Jesus Christ, true God and man, is truly, really, and substantially contained under the perceptible species of bread and win. It is not contradictory to say that our Savior always sits at the right hand of the Father in heaven according to his natural way of existing and that, nevertheless, in his substance he is sacramentally present in many other places with us. We can hardly find words to express this way of existing; but our reason, guided by faith, can know that it is possible for God, and this we should always believe unhesitatingly. For all our predecessors in the true Church of Christ who treated of this most holy sacrament very clearly professed that our Redeemer instituted this wonderful sacrament at the Last Supper, when, after he had blessed bread and win, he said in plain, unmistakable words that he was giving them his own body and his own blood. These words are recorded by the

Evangelists and afterwards repeated by St. Paul. These words have their proper and obvious meaning and were so understood by the Fathers. Consequently, it is indeed an infamy that contentious, evil men should distort these words into fanciful, imaginary figures of speech that deny the truth about the body and blood of Christ, contrary to the universal understanding of the Church. The Church, the pillar and mainstay of the truth, has detested these satanical falsehoods that evil men have invented, and it accepts with unfailing gratitude this marvelous gift from the hands of Christ.

Thoughts to ponder

"In Cana of Galilee, Christ changed water into wine, and shall we think Him less worthy of credit when He changes wine into His Blood?"- St. Cyril of Jerusalem

"Since Christ Himself has said: "*This is My Body*" – who shall dare to doubt that It is His Body?" –St. Cyril of Jerusalem

"Whereas in the Lord's Prayer, we are bidden to ask for 'our daily bread', the Holy Fathers of the Church all but unanimously teach that by these words must be understood, not so much that material bread which is the support of the body, as the Eucharistic bread, which ought to be our daily food." – Pope St. Pius X

MARY

And the wine failing, the mother of Jesus saith to him: They have no wine. And Jesus saith to her: Woman, what is that to me and to thee? My hour is not yet come. (John 2:3-4)

Interpretation

Christ didn't like His mother commanding Him so he chose a public place to rebuke her and to stress His independence.

Consider this

* Christ, being God, gave the Ten Commandments. Do you think it is possible that Christ would is not subject to the commandment of honoring your father and mother? If Christ, who is to be an example to us, doesn't have to follow the commandments He gave us then why should Christ expect us to follow them after His example? Christ does obey His mother in John 2:7.

* Mary is indeed the mother of Christ for why else would Elizabeth say, "And whence this is to me that the mother of my Lord should come to me" (Luke 1:43)? Mary was the mother of Christ as man, but not as God. However, since the humanity and divinity of Christ are joined and inseparable it is indeed proper for Mary to be called mother.

* Mary only had one child. The word "brethren" is often termed as the word "brother". However, in that part of the world "brethren" refers to cousins because they consider their cousins to be brothers and sisters. When they come to visit countries that use the word "cousin" they often find it a difficult concept to understand. This is not my definition, nor is it the Catholic Church's; this is an anthropology term (you may check this out with an anthropology teacher).

* Christ was the firstborn son of Mary. Therefore, people claim that she had to have more. However, any child who was born first can be considered the first born. If we can accept people today, of only having one child in which they call their first born, why is it difficult to accept Christ as an only child? Also, in Hebrews 1:6 St. Paul talks about Christ being the first begotten. Does this mean that there are other sons of God?

* People also claim that Mary and St. Joseph had a normal relationship after the birth of Christ. For those who believe in the Bible only this is difficult to prove because there is nothing relating to what kind of relationship they had. Also, there are some who claim that Joseph was previously married and that he brought in children from that marriage; again this is hard to prove based upon the Bible alone because there is nothing to support this.

* It is often mentioned that Christ had the following as brothers: Sts. James, Joseph, Simon and Jude (Matthew 13:55). In the same verse the people say "Is not this the carpenter's son?" and not "is this not one of the carpenter's sons?" In Matthew 10:3-4 it shows that James is the son of either Zebedee or Alpheus

(depending on which one you are talking about), Simon is from Canan, not Nazareth or Bethlehem and Jude is the brother of James (Luke 6:16). In Mark 15:40 it says that James the less and Joseph were brothers and therefore could not be actual brothers of Christ.

Some will say that Christ had sisters. There are no names mentioned and therefore, again it is difficult to prove by the Bible alone.

*How great is Mary? In Luke 1:42 St. Elizabeth speaks of Mary "Blessed art thou among women." Many non-Catholics will say that Mary is great among women but isn't above women. The word 'blessed' is used as an adjective to describe the subject you, which is Mary. It is not used to describe women. One can then change the order of words to show this to show that Mary is above women and not just among them: for example 'You are blessed among women' or 'Among women you are blessed.' Therefore, while Mary can be called great among women she is to be held higher than all. In Luke 1:48 she says of herself "for behold henceforth all generations shall call me blessed." Notice she didn't say "this generation" or "the next generation" but "all generations." For there is no other woman in the Bible that stakes this claim for herself. Only Mary will be called blessed for all generations from her time forward.

*Since Christ is implied to be the second Adam (Roman 5:14-15) there also must be a second Eve. It was Eve who cooperated with the Devil and brought sin into the world; since she is considered the mother of all living things (Genesis 3:20) along with being the mother of us in sin there also must be a mother of all who will cooperate with God and be the mother of us in grace.

For if Eve was created without sin and fell from grace then the new Eve must also be without sin and never fall from grace. Once sin had entered into the world all must suffer the effects of it and when we fall from grace we become allies with the Devil and an enemy of God. Therefore, this new Eve must be born without original sin, be full of grace from the very beginning of life and never commit a sin before her earthly death. In Luke 1:28 the angel says to Mary “Hail, full of grace, the Lord is with thee: blessed art thou among women.” Here we see two things: first is that she is full of grace and therefore with the stain of original sin. But if one says that their bible says “favored one” then that would show that she must have had the stain of sin on her and therefore the Devil can claim that he had power over the Mother of God and even God Himself.

STATUES AND SAINTS

Thou shalt not have strange gods before me. Thou shalt not make to thyself a graven thing, nor the likeness of anything that is in the heaven above, or in the earth beneath, nor of those things that are I the waters under the earth. (Exodus 20:3-4)

Interpretation

This shows and proves that Catholics are idol worshiping and are not true Christians. Catholic have statues which they pray to and reward when they get something. Also, this is a call to action to destroy all images such as photographs and statues of loved ones and famous people or anyone else we admire or whose virtues we would like to imitate.

Consider this

* Anyone that prays to a statue, expecting something, is indeed guilty of idol worshipping. For that person is expecting and believes that that statue is powerful and will grant whatever the person wants. Catholics do not pray to the statue but in front of them for they realize that the statue is nothing more than a representation of the person to whom they are praying to.

* If having images (statues, relics, pictures, etc) to remember heaven is wrong then why does God command and approve it? In Exodus 25 (and soon after the Ten Commandments were given) God gives Moses directions to make a sanctuary, the Ark of the Covenant, candlesticks, etc. In Numbers 21:8 God again commands Moses to make a brazen serpent; at the dedication of Solomon's temple God resided there as a cloud (3 Kings 8:10-12).

* If it is wrong for Catholics to have statues of whom they honor then it also must be wrong for people to place statues in parks, buildings, etc. and even to have photographs of loved ones. It will be said that there is a difference between the two which is that statues and photographs of famous people and loved ones are there to help remind people of who they are or what they did. Catholics will claim the same rights about statues and relics of religious people whom they honor.

* It is also claimed that by praying to the saints we are taking away from the glory that is God alone. If one would listen to the prayers of a Catholic one would hear the words, while praying to a saint, "pray for us," and when a Catholic prays to God one would hear "have mercy on us." We go to the saints because we know that they are in Heaven and are friends of God. When we pray we ask that they go to God on our behalf, because we are sinners and fall short of the glory of God, and request some favor for us; we never ask the saints to grant anything because only God has the power to do so.

The Church teaches

from the Council of Trent, 1545-63

Further, the images of Christ, of the Virgin Mother of God, and of other saints are to be kept with honor in places of worship especially; and to them due honor and veneration is to be paid- not because it is believed that there is any divinity or power intrinsic to them for which they are reverenced, nor because it is from them that something is sought, nor that a blind trust is to be attached to images as it once was by the Gentiles who placed their hope in idols; but because the honor which is shown to them is referred to the prototypes which they represent. Thus, it follows that through these images which we kiss and before which we kneel and uncover our heads, we are adoring Christ and venerating the saints whose likeness these images bear.

Thoughts to ponder

"The saints must be honored as friends of Christ and children and heirs of God. Let us carefully observe the manner of life of all the apostles, martyrs, ascetics, and just men who announced the coming of the Lord. And let us emulate their faith, charity, hope, zeal, life, patience under suffering, and perseverance unto death so that we may also share their crowns of glory." - St. John Damascus

“When we enter ornate and clean Basilicas, adorned with crosses, sacred images, altars and burning lamps, we most easily conceive devotion. But on the other hand, when we enter the temple of heretics, where there is nothing except a chair for preaching and a table for making a meal, we feel ourselves to be entering a profane hall and not the House of God.”

–St. Robert Bellarmine

Final Thoughts

Dear reader, it is time for us to depart from this crossroad and to continue our own separate journeys. Before we leave I have one other gift for you: I offer you the sword that pierced Mary's heart so that thoughts may be revealed. I give it to you so that you may not only remember this meeting but also to ward off the dangers that could befall you if you ever stray off the path of salvation.

As I have said before it has never been my intention to explain all what the Church has taught but rather to give you some thoughts and considerations of what is and isn't true. Now, as you continue your journey you will have something to think about for you are bound to seek and know the truth.

Mark my words well and heed this advice: If you seek the truth in both research and prayers you shall find it sooner or later; if you live the truth you shall die in the truth. However, if you find the truth and reject it you shall die without truth. Remember: "The lips of the just teach many; but they that are ignorant, shall die in the want of understanding." (Proverbs 10:21)

Now let us depart as friends and pray for each other that we may both see each other again, perhaps at another crossroad and in Heaven.

Dóminus vobíscum

www.ingramcontent.com/pod-product-compliance
Ingram Content Group UK Ltd.
Pitfield, Milton Keynes, MK11 3LW, UK
UKHW022019190726
13853UKWH00005B/2013

9 789887 703990